Money Matters

Luis Angeles

Money Matters

How Money and Banks Evolved, and Why We
Have Financial Crises

Luis Angeles
Adam Smith Business School
University of Glasgow
Glasgow, UK

ISBN 978-3-030-95515-1   ISBN 978-3-030-95516-8   (eBook)
https://doi.org/10.1007/978-3-030-95516-8

Cover illustration: © Melisa Hasan

This Palgrave Macmillan imprint is published by the registered company Springer Nature Switzerland AG
The registered company address is: Gewerbestrasse 11, 6330 Cham, Switzerland

La difficulté est une monnaie que les savants emploient pour ne découvrir la vanité de leur art, et de laquelle l'humaine bêtise se paie aisément.

Michel de Montaigne, Essays, Book II, Chapter 12

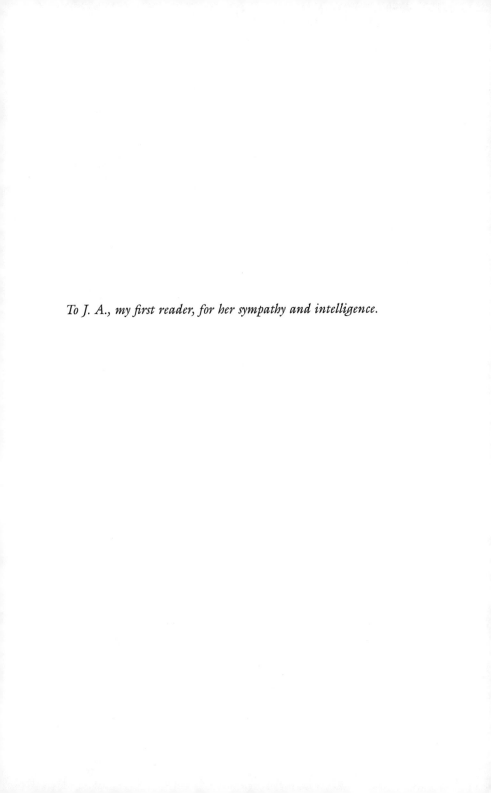

To J. A., my first reader, for her sympathy and intelligence.

CONTENTS

About the Author

Luis Angeles is Professor of Economics at the Adam Smith Business School of the University of Glasgow, United Kingdom. He has published work in economic history, economic development, and banking and financial topics. His work has appeared in academic journals such as *The Economic History Review*, *Explorations in Economic History*, the *Journal of Development Economics*, the *European Economic Review*, *Economica*, *Kyklos*, and more. He has held numerous leadership positions in academia, and is currently a Head of Subject for Economics.

LIST OF FIGURES

CHAPTER 1

Introduction

Among the many peculiarities of economics as an academic discipline, the following may be the most curious one. Economics is understood by the non-specialist as a subject deeply concerned with money and money-related phenomena. Which experts are sought by the media to comment on problems of inflation, debt, or financial crises? Economists, of course. At the same time, and unbeknown to the general public, a firmly held conviction runs across the corpus of scholarly work in the discipline. This conviction, so fundamental that a majority of economists hardly ever ponders its validity, is the idea that, except for some superficial considerations, *money does not matter*.

At some point during their academic formation, typically after having mastered the core areas of the subject, students of economics are offered a course on a specialized topic whose name must seem puzzling to the uninitiated: "monetary economics". As it turns out, monetary economics is a specialized branch of the subject dedicated to the study of economic phenomena in an environment where money is present. A moment of reflection would then lead to a rather startling conclusion. If a specialized branch of the subject has been established to study economic phenomena when money is present, it follows that the rest of the subject—and therefore the vast majority of work produced by economists over the last two centuries—is done under alternative environments. The vast majority of economics, then, must be non-monetary: the study of economic

L. Angeles, *Money Matters*, https://doi.org/10.1007/978-3-030-95516-8_1

phenomena under the assumption that money does not exist. As students of the subject will know, this conclusion happens to be absolutely right.

Sometime during the early to mid-nineteenth century, economists convinced themselves that money is a topic of minor importance for the discipline, and that most economic analysis can be performed better by imagining an economy where money does not exist. The principle was established well enough by the year 1848, when John Stuart Mill's *Principles of Political Economy*, possibly the earliest textbook on the subject and certainly one the most influential ever, was published in its first edition. In a chapter titled "On money", Mill advances what had become by then a widely held conviction: "There cannot, in short, be intrinsically a more insignificant thing, in the economy of society, than money" (Mill 1848, Book II, Chapter VII). One hundred and seventy years later, this fundamental principle continues to rule the profession.

To be sure, there is a logic underlying the economists' assertion that money does not matter. Not only have I nothing against these arguments, I find they provide valuable insights into the workings of all economies. Economists point out that the wealth of any society, the quantity of goods and services available for the consumption of its members, is ultimately not related to the quantity of money available. Societies are rich because they have a lot of productive resources such as people, machinery and raw materials, together with the knowledge of how to put these resources to use in the production of final goods and services. Societies get richer by producing more, and they produce more by expanding their knowledge or by accumulating productive resources in the form of more people with a good education, more modern machinery, better infrastructure, and so on. Societies cannot get richer simply by creating more money. Money, in this long-term perspective, only facilitates the exchange of goods and services. The production of goods and services is not related to it.

Unfortunately, from this correct observation about the ultimate drivers of economic development, economists derived a doctrine which they proceeded to apply to economic analysis across the board. The doctrine is called *monetary neutrality*, and simply states that money has no bearing on any economic outcome of consequence. All that money does, according to this doctrine, is determine the level of prices—twice as much money in circulation would lead to prices twice as large, with no change on the things that really matter such as employment levels, production, consumption of goods and services, and so on. The main implication of this was ably summarized by Joseph A. Schumpeter, one of the leading economists of the twentieth century. In his words, acceptance of money neutrality implies that "[n]ot only *can* [money] be discarded whenever we are analyzing the fundamental features of the economic process but it *must* be discarded just as a veil must be drawn aside if we are to see the face behind it" (Schumpeter 1954, p. 277, italics in the original). The metaphor of money as a veil, obscuring a pure view of the economic process, is one of the most enduring motifs in the discipline.

This, then, explains the absence of money from most economic analysis. Economic models are mathematical constructions in which households and firms are assumed to exchange labour, capital, and final goods and services directly—without intervening monetary payments. The principle is taken to extremes that the lay person would find difficult to believe. Banks are routinely studied within models that do not feature money, where they are understood as institutions that transfer real resources between agents in the economy. And quite elaborate reasons are found to make sense of financial crises in a world where money would be absent.

This book starts from the principle that the above position is mistaken—in other words, that *money matters*. Money may not be a determinant of long-run economic development, but monetary neutrality does not follow from that fact. Money is an integral part of the economic process, and we cannot hope to understand the economy if we chose to leave it out of the picture. I believe that money, and more specifically the processes in place to create and remove money from society, matter a great deal to economic outcomes. I believe the study of banks and financial crises only makes sense if money is front and center. And I believe that large swathes of the economics corpus will need to be rewritten from scratch to take money realistically into consideration.

A great way to begin mending the above problems is by studying the history of money and banking—the topic of the first part of the present book. Understanding how money and banks evolved is important for reasons that go well beyond the acquisition of a historical perspective from which to analyse present-day phenomena. In my opinion, the history of money is the best way to approach fundamental questions about the nature of money and banks—questions such as "what is money?", "what do banks do?", and "how does money creation take place?". No discussion of monetary phenomena can go far without these questions showing up, and any person with an interest in money and financial matters would do well to tackle them early on.

The second part of the book aims to demonstrate the benefits of acquiring the knowledge offered in the first part by putting it to work on a topic of much importance for present-day societies: the occurrence of financial crises. We will search to understand what financial crises are, why they happen, and what we can do about them. Financial crises seem difficult to understand only because we misunderstand money and banking. Get money and banking right and, as I hope to demonstrate, the mechanics of financial crises opens before our eyes.

A final word on method. The reader will find this book eschews jargon and technical language, and does not employ mathematical formulation. Maths is wonderful but, in the social sciences, quite often misused to give the appearance of insight when there is none. As once stated by John Kenneth Galbraith, another towering figure of the discipline during the twentieth century, "[T]here are no useful propositions in economics that cannot be stated in clear, unembellished and generally agreeable English".[1] Galbraith's dictum flies in the face of most of what is produced in academia today, whether in economics or beyond. A very good reason, then, to try to live up to its challenge.

---

[1] Galbraith (1987, p. 4). Arguably, languages other than English would also do.

CHAPTER 2

What Is Money?

Keywords Money · Currency · Money supply · Bank deposits · Money creation

Mr. Paul Dombey, wealthy businessman living in England during Victorian times, was more than a little surprised with the impromptu question of his five-year-old son, Master Paul Dombey, one evening by the fire:

'Papa! what's money?'
[...]
'What is money, Paul?' he answered. 'Money?'
'Yes,' said the child, laying his hands upon the elbows of his little chair, and turning the old face up towards Mr Dombey's; 'what is money?'
Mr Dombey was in a difficulty. He would have liked to give him some explanation involving the terms circulating-medium, currency, depreciation of currency, paper, bullion, rates of exchange, value of precious metals in the market, and so forth; but looking down at the little chair, and seeing what a long way down it was, he answered: 'Gold, and silver, and copper. Guineas, shillings, half-pence. You know what they are?'
'Oh yes, I know what they are,' said Paul. 'I don't mean that Papa. I mean what's money after all?'
Charles Dickens, *Dombey and Son*

© The Author(s), under exclusive license to Springer Nature Switzerland AG 2022
L. Angeles, *Money Matters*,
https://doi.org/10.1007/978-3-030-95516-8_2

Difficult task for Mr. Dombey. The question addressed to him is far more complex than it first appears. What is money? To be sure, money is cash, the coins and banknotes we carry in our wallets—the "[g]uineas, shillings, half-pence" of Victorian England. We have no problem recognizing such items as money since we handle them on a daily basis, and regularly use them to pay others for goods and services. What is more, coins and banknotes are produced by a central government—or by a public institution under central government oversight. This reinforces our assurance that they are money, since they somehow carry with them the guarantee and support of the state.

And yet, as young Master Dombey seems to have realized quite beyond his years, there is more to money than coins and banknotes.

A good way to think about money is as that which is always accepted as payment for goods and services in an economy. Money allows you to buy anything that is for sale, and is accepted by a seller regardless of the identity of the buyer. This universal acceptability relies on a self-reinforcing logic: I will accept a form of payment from you because I believe it will be accepted by other people later on, when it will be my turn to offer it as payment. In other words, people are willing to accept a given means of payment precisely because it is so widely accepted.

Coins and banknotes are certainly money but, at the same time, the vast majority of payments taking place in any modern economy are not settled with them. Experience tells us that we use coins and banknotes chiefly for small purchases—to pay for a coffee or a restaurant bill, for a bus or a taxi ride. For anything more consequential, and increasingly even for small payments as well, we use our debit cards— or some other method that authorizes a debit on a bank deposit in our name and a corresponding credit on a bank deposit in the name of the seller. The practice dispenses with the inconvenience of carrying cash for both buyer and seller; it is safer, leaner, and altogether more convenient. When we make such a transaction we say we are paying with money, even though no physical object is changing hands. What, then, is money when, as is the case in most transactions, no coins or banknotes are being transferred? What is money when we make payments which involve our bank deposits?

To be able to answer we need to understand what bank deposits are. Nearly every adult in every advanced economy is the owner of a bank deposit, and uses it regularly to make payments. You would expect an item of such ubiquity to be well understood by the public, but that is far from being the case. Bank deposits are commonly misunderstood and, given their importance, they are the perfect place to start in our quest to understand money better.

That people are bewildered by the nature of bank deposits is in fact not surprising. To see why, I will ask you to consider a transaction which you may not necessarily be familiar with, but which will serve us to bring the nature of bank deposits into evidence. Let us refer to all forms of money which are produced by the state or by a state-sponsored institution as *currency*—the coins and banknotes we have mentioned above. The transaction I will ask you to consider is the deposit, at a bank, of an item *other* than currency.

Indeed, money in currency form is not the only type of valuable which you may hand over to a bank. Many banks offer the service of accepting deposits of valuable items such as jewelry, art objects, documents in their original form, and so on. These items are kept in special storage boxes within the bank's vault, and are therefore protected by all the security systems the bank has to offer. Each storage box contains items belonging to one, and only one, client. Let us refer to this type of transaction as a "regular deposit".

I bring this transaction to the fore because the temptation is great to regard a deposit of currency as just a regular deposit where the item being deposited happens to be currency. That is not the case—if you bring currency to a bank for deposit, the bank will not be keeping this currency in storage. Depositing currency at a bank results in a legal agreement which is of a completely different nature to the one that arises when we deposit other valuables. When we deposit a valuable other than currency, the bank agrees to hold the item in question under custody, ensure its safety, and render it back to us on demand. The bank can never use the item, loan it to somebody else, or profit from it in any way. Without a shadow of a doubt, the ownership of the item has not changed: it continues to belong to us. The bank charges a fee for this service, which is the service of keeping something in a safe place.

When we bring currency to a bank in order to establish a bank deposit, however, something very different happens. The bank simply takes the currency and, in return, issues a debt against itself and in our favour. A deposit of currency, then, is no deposit at all—in the sense that you are not placing your currency at the bank for the purpose of it being held safely in custody. Instead, you are transferring ownership of your currency to the bank—it is not your currency anymore from the moment you deposit it. In exchange for this transfer of ownership, the bank is recognizing a debt towards you which is payable at any time, on demand. We call these debts bank deposits.

A few observations follow from the above. The operation we refer to as "withdrawing money from a bank deposit" is nothing other than asking the bank to pay some of the debt it owes to us—the bank pays back its debt by giving us currency. And when you make a payment using your bank deposit, what effectively happens is that the bank reduces its debt towards you and increases its debt towards somebody else. In other words, a payment using bank deposits is a transfer of debt—the buyer in the transaction authorizes some of the debt owed to him to be transferred in favour of the seller. When we offer to pay for something by means of our debit card, we are asking our counterparty to accept a debt from a bank as a payment for the goods or services on offer. Here, then, is the answer to the question posed by young Master Dombey at the beginning of this chapter.

What is money? Money is two things: currency and bank deposits. Currency is objects made of metal or paper issued by a public authority which we all agree to accept as payment in economic transactions. And bank deposits are debts. More specifically, they are debts issued by private commercial banks in favour of the public which are payable on demand in the form of currency. These debts are almost universally accepted as a form of payment in all economic transactions—hence, they are money. The vast majority of transactions in any modern economy are settled using bank deposits and they are, effectively, the only acceptable form of money when large sums are involved—only criminals make large payments with suitcases full of currency. Most of the money in circulation is in the form of bank deposits which, of course, means that most money in circulation is nothing other than debts.

~~~

The total quantity of money in an economy is an important magnitude which economists call the money supply. The money supply is the sum of all currency in circulation and all bank deposits, and we may quantify the total value of each of these two components.

When we do so, it becomes clear that the vast majority of the money which people hold and use is in the form of bank deposits. Take the United Kingdom, for example. On the 30th of June 2019 the money supply of the country amounted to 2.43 trillion British pounds. On that

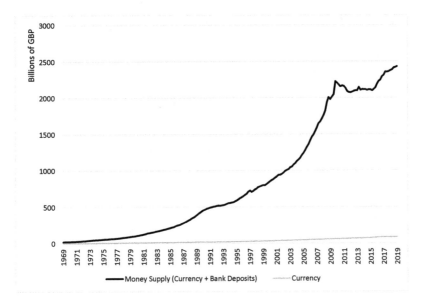

Fig. 2.1 The money supply of the United Kingdom, 1969–2019 (*Source* Bank of England)

same day, all currency in circulation was worth a comparatively measly 82.8 billion pounds—or about 3.4% of the total.

The United Kingdom is by no means an outlier in this context. In country after country, and most particularly in all advanced economies, we are bound to find the same thing: currency is far less important than bank deposits in the composition of the money supply. The precise percentage will vary from country to country, but the general point holds. In accordance with the personal experience of most readers, the vast majority of money in all modern economies is in the form of bank deposits.

Among the few things that can be said about the money supply with a high degree of confidence is that it tends to grow. A larger economy needs more money, and economic growth is typically accompanied by growth in the quantity of money in circulation. In all modern economies, and save for some exceptional circumstances, the money supply is each year larger than the previous year.

Figure 2.1 illustrates this fact with the case of the United Kingdom, by plotting the evolution of all money in circulation between June 1969 and

June 2019. Over this 50-year period, the money supply of the United Kingdom grew at an average rate of 9.8% per year—from £23 billion in 1969 to the £2.43 trillion of 2019 already mentioned. This 100-fold increase in the quantity of money available was considerably larger than the increase in the size of the British economy over the same period of time (a 45-fold increase when measured in nominal terms). Money has become ever more abundant.

Figure 2.1 also shows that the British money supply suffered a spectacular change of tendency shortly after the year 2008. Having grown pretty much continuously over the previous forty years, it decreased substantially and then remained stagnant for several years in a row. This period corresponds to the aftermath of the global financial crisis of 2008, and the changes we observe will be discussed at length in the second part of this book. Let us defer that discussion entirely, and focus on the evolution of money over the long run instead.

Over the long run, the quantity of money available in the economy grows and, in addition, its composition changes. Figure 2.1 illustrates this by plotting the evolution of currency in the United Kingdom, alongside the evolution of the money supply. Since money is currency plus bank deposits, the quantity of bank deposits in the economy can be read as the difference between the two lines. As the figure makes clear, the two lines grow further and further away from each other. Albeit this will not be obvious from the figure, currency was 15% of the total money supply back in 1969. The percentage steadily declines over the subsequent decades, reaching less than 5% by the late 1980s and around 3.5% nowadays. A similar tendency towards a growing importance of bank deposits with respect to currency will be observed in all advanced economies over long enough periods of time.

Figure 2.1, then, illustrates a simple reality. Additional money is created, for a value of many billions of pounds, dollars or euros, in every modern economy year after year. Some of this additional money is in the form of currency, but most is in the form of bank deposits. How does all this money creation take place?

When it comes to currency, money creation seems easy enough to understand. Currency is literally manufactured by the Central Bank, a public institution under the oversight of the central government. The Central Bank has a monopoly over the production of currency, and whoever tries to put fake banknotes into circulation is guilty of a serious crime. Because of this, we are accustomed to think of money creation by private actors as unlawful, and morally wrong.

As has been noted, however, most money in circulation is in the form of bank deposits and bank deposits are nothing other than bank debts. We must thus admit that the vast majority of money in any modern economy has been created not by the public sector, but by the commercial banking sector. And not only that. The process whereby banks create all this money and put it into circulation is, as it turns out, largely unknown to the vast majority of people.

How are bank deposits created? The common sense answer is that, as the name indicates, bank deposits are created when members of the public bring currency into banks for deposit. And indeed, only a few paragraphs above I have myself argued that banks issue a debt we call a bank deposit upon reception of currency. End of story, right?

Unfortunately, no. A deposit of currency at a bank does result in the creation of a bank deposit, but this mechanism can never lead to a net increase in the aggregate quantity of bank deposits in the economy. This seems counterintuitive but isn't—allow me to elaborate.

In all modern economies, there is only one available method for the public to obtain currency: withdrawal from an already existing bank deposit. If you have currency in your hands, you have either withdrawn it from your bank using an ATM or other similar procedure, or you have received it from another person who has performed this operation beforehand (or who received it from another person who did it, etc.). You can be sure this is the case because all currency in circulation is physically produced by the Central Bank, and it is illegal for the Central Bank to transfer any of this currency to the public or to a government agency. If such a transfer was possible, the public would be able to obtain currency by selling goods or services to the Central Bank or to the government, and be paid with freshly printed banknotes. It is precisely to avoid potential abuses that these operations are rendered unfeasible.

What, then, does the Central Bank do with the currency it produces—and how does it finish in our hands? The answer is that the Central Bank sells the currency to commercial banks. Commercial banks buy this currency by offering financial assets in return—typically, bonds which have been previously issued by the government, and which commercial banks have acquired.[1] Thus, banks exchange an interest-paying asset such as a bond for an asset which pays no interest and is costly to keep, namely currency. Why do they do this? Because they need the currency to comply with the promise they make to bank deposit owners: that any deposit will be paid on demand and in the form of currency. Notice that this only makes sense if banks have created bank deposits without first receiving currency—but let's not run ahead of ourselves. For the moment we have established that currency reaches the public via banks and, as a consequence, that the public can only increase its holdings of currency by decreasing its holdings of bank deposits by the same amount. From this, two conclusions must follow.

First, we can only deposit currency which has been previously withdrawn from the banking system. A withdrawal of currency is the reverse operation of a currency deposit: just as handing currency to a bank results in the creation of a bank deposit, withdrawals from a bank result in the destruction of a bank deposit for the amount withdrawn. Thus, any deposit of currency is effectively reinstating a bank deposit which had been previously destroyed. When we take into account the withdrawal which, by necessity, must have preceded the deposit, the net effect on the quantity of bank deposits in the economy is zero.

And there is more. We cannot deposit currency which we have not previously withdrawn from a bank, but we *can* withdraw currency from a bank and fail to deposit it back into the banking system. In fact, that is what most of us do. Recall from Fig. 2.1 that the total value of currency in circulation grows from year to year. The only way in which that can happen is for currency withdrawals to exceed currency deposits for the average person in the economy, year after year. Surely your own personal experience corroborates this notion. Most of us withdraw currency from our bank deposits with some regularity, albeit in small amounts. On the other hand, when was the last time you made a deposit of currency? Far from increasing the overall amount of bank deposits in the economy, the public's pattern of currency withdrawals and deposits typically reduces it.

By this point, you may be thinking the situation resembles a chicken-and-egg problem. A deposit of currency creates a bank deposit, but the currency must be obtained from an already existing bank deposit in the

---

[1] A bond is nothing other than a debt which can be bought and sold in a market. Most debts, including the debts we owe to banks, are not regularly traded and are therefore not bonds.

first place—how was that first bank deposit created? And if people withdraw more currency than they deposit, how come the total quantity of bank deposits in the economy keeps growing year after year? The answer to both questions is simple, and is my second conclusion. There must exist an additional mechanism, other than the deposit of currency at a bank, that leads to bank deposit creation. This additional mechanism must be responsible for *all* the net growth in aggregate bank deposits we observe year after year.

This last conclusion should surprise you. Money is an essential feature of everyday life, something we are all intimately acquainted with. Earning money, spending money, investing our money, are all part of every person's experience. And yet, before reading the present chapter you were perhaps not quite aware that most of the money in circulation is nothing other than bank debts. And, now that you know it, you realize that most of these debts are created through a process you cannot begin to describe. Money creation is central to the functioning of all economies, yet it seems that hardly anyone knows how it happens.

~~~

With characteristic wit, John Kenneth Galbraith once remarked that "[t]he process by which banks create money is so simple that the mind is repelled. When something so important is involved, a deeper mystery seems only decent."[2] I believe Galbraith was quite right saying this and, for our purposes, it represents a problem. The process of money creation by banks is indeed surprisingly simple—so much so, in fact, that if I were to offer you a straightforward explanation at this point you would, in all likelihood, misunderstand me or disbelieve me. I teach economics at university, I know what I'm talking about.

Knowing this, I want to take a less direct approach. I believe the best way to arrive at a solid understanding not just of money creation, but of money and banking in general, is by explaining how money and banks evolved since their earliest manifestations in human history. In other words, I intend to tell you not just how the monetary system works, but also why it came to work the way it does. Most of the features of today's

---

[2] Galbraith (1975, p. 22).

monetary system only make sense when looked at from a historical view-point—you would not design the current system the way it is, if design had been possible. The next few chapters, then, offer the reader a history of money and banking.

For this detour into history, I offer no apology. The very best economics transitions from history to empirical analysis and from empir-ical analysis to theory seamlessly and unapologetically—as shown by Adam Smith, right at the beginnings of the discipline. Us economists could hardly do better than to follow the master.

PART I

A History of Money and Banking

CHAPTER 3

Money from the Very Beginning

Keywords Unit of account · Barter · Bilateral debts · Coinage · Precious metal · Debasement

Money can be a nebulous concept, the more so the further back in time we research its origins. Money only becomes recognizable to our eyes with the invention of coinage, sometime towards the end of the seventh century BC. Coins, after all, are objects universally accepted as a means of payment—our usual definition of money. In this chapter, however, I will encourage you to think not so much in terms of money, but in terms of monetary systems. A monetary system may be loosely defined as a set of arrangements which societies have in place to measure the value of goods and services and to carry out exchange. Objects to which we attach the label of "money" may well be part of the monetary system but, surprisingly to modern eyes, they don't have to.

The two millennia that preceded the invention of coinage saw the development of large and complex societies in ancient Mesopotamia, Egypt, and throughout the Middle East.[1] Albeit these societies did not

---

[1] Obviously, complex societies developed in numerous other places, but my account focuses on Europe and the Middle East. Modern forms of money were invented in Europe, and were then adopted throughout the world.

L. Angeles, *Money Matters*, https://doi.org/10.1007/978-3-030-95516-8_3

17

have a single object which was universally employed as a means of payment in all transactions, they most definitely measured the value of things and carried out economic exchange. In other words, they did not have money as is commonly understood, but they did have a monetary system. It will be pertinent for us to understand how such a system worked.

The first step in the monetary development of societies comes with the introduction of what historians of money call a *unit of account*. A unit of account is a quantity of economic value, in terms of which we can express the value of all goods and services in an economy. This makes the value of all items comparable, and makes possible the handling of debts. Debts expressed in terms of the unit of account can be added and subtracted from each other, and interest payments can be calculated on them. In a very meaningful sense, a unit of account turns a pre-monetary society into a monetary one, and makes complex social organization possible.

Albeit we cannot say for sure, units of account were most likely an invention of the very first state bureaucracies established in human societies. By the time written records arrive, during the 3rd millennium BC in ancient Mesopotamia, we see units of account in regular use to record debts owed to or by the state, as well as calculations regarding these debts. Since all states tax and spend, and the timing of taxes does not match the timing of expenditures, state organization requires debt management—which in turn requires a unit of account.

The most straightforward method for introducing a unit of account is to define it as the value of one unit of some well-known or prestigious commodity. Ancient Mesopotamia, for instance, used the value of one measure of barley and the value of one measure of silver as units of account—two units of account were in place, and were used interchangeably. It is important to note that the value of barley or the value of silver were not determined in a market, as would be the case today. It is unlikely that such markets existed and, if they did, the prices determined in them would be volatile—not what we want when looking for a stable standard of value. Instead, the value of barley and silver in terms of a range of goods and services (and in terms of each other) was determined by decree: the state declared it, and then enforced it in all transactions on which it was involved. The public was then able to adopt these units in order to price goods in private transactions, as well as when establishing private debts.

Defining the unit of account as the value of one unit of some well-known or prestigious commodity has a notable advantage: the commodity in question can be used as a means of payment whenever available and convenient. Thus, if the value of a sheep is set at one hundred measures of barley, it is in principle possible for a person to buy a sheep by offering one hundred measures of actual barley in exchange. Notice, however, that this exchange is possible but not necessary. The buyer may not have any barley to offer or, if he does, the seller may not be willing to accept it. A number of reasons may be advanced for a refusal to be paid in barley: maybe the seller has no storage place for it, maybe she will be travelling and cannot take it with her, and so on. A unit of account allows all goods and services to be priced and compared, but it does not prescribe the use of any particular means of payment.

Ancient societies, then, had a unit of account but they did not have money—there was no item universally accepted as a means of payment and present in all transactions. Goods and services were priced in terms of the units of account, and transactions were recorded as involving a value of such and such units of barley or such and such units of silver—but in most cases barley or silver did not exchange hands. People bought and sold goods and services from each other in the absence of money—the question is, how?

Economists tend to answer this question by referring to a folktale that has been transmitted from generation to generation since formulated in its most memorable form by Adam Smith, back in the year 1776. The tale says that before the invention of money, understood as an object universally accepted in payments for goods and services, exchange was regularly carried out via *barter*. In other words, people simply swapped the goods or services they had in excess for those they had a need of, agreeing on a rate of exchange between the items in question on a case by case basis. Adam Smith was one of the brightest minds ever to employ itself in the service of economics but, on this occasion, he got it almost entirely wrong.

As we now know, the idea that, at some point in the past, exchange within societies was organized mainly by means of barter is false. The evidence has been in place for several decades, and was collected by anthropologists, observing present-day societies living in a primitive stage of monetary development, and by economic historians, researching past societies living in diverse stages of monetary development. Their conclusions could hardly have been any clearer. Here, for instance, are the words of George Dalton, a leading figure in anthropology, summarizing the findings of this academic field of study back in 1982:

> Barter, in the strict sense of moneyless market exchange, has never been a quantitatively important or dominant model of transaction in any past or present economic system about which we have hard information.
>
> As a minor, infrequent, petty, or emergency transaction, barter occurs widely in past and present economies.
>
> [...]
>
> ... wherever barter exists, so too do non-barter alternatives, which are always known to the barter participants and which are quantitatively much more important in the larger economic system in which the petty or infrequent barter transactions occur.
>
> Dalton (1982, pp. 185–186)[2]

Barter has been often recorded between people from different societies meeting casually or irregularly—for instance, European explorers visiting islands in the Pacific. Among members of a society, however, barter is "minor, infrequent, petty" and an "emergency transaction"—even in the absence of money. What, then, is the typical method for carrying out transactions in societies that do not have money? The answer is simple yet revealing: before the introduction of money, and in most places even after the introduction of money whenever money was scarce, most economic exchange was carried out by establishing bilateral debts, and subsequently cancelling such debts against each other.

As an example, imagine John buys food and drink from Jane's grocery store for a value of £100 and, instead of paying with cash which would be either inexistent or rarely available, he issues a debt against himself and in favour of Jane for that value. At a later date, Jane obtains plumbing services from John for her home for a value of £80, likewise issuing a debt instead of paying with cash. Later still, John and Jane meet in order to cancel out each other's debts—establishing that John only needs to pay Jane £20 in cash. Thus, goods and services would have been exchanged for a value of £180, yet only £20 worth of cash was employed in the process. And of course, John's net debt of £20 could still be carried forward, and cancelled out against future debts to be established in both directions—reducing the requirement for money in the exchange process towards zero.

---

[2] For more on the topic of barter and its lack of importance in societies studied by anthropology see Humphrey (1985) and Graeber (2011, Chapter 2).

We have evidence that exchange of this kind was in place from the earliest civilizations in the Middle East to the eighteenth century in Europe, and that most exchange was organized this way in most times and places.[3] The historian Craig Muldrew has estimated that over 90% of all transactions were carried out without using money in seventeenth century England—a society where coinage had been in circulation at least since Roman times.[4]

To give an image of how the system worked on a social-wide scale, consider the following description by legal historian Emily Kadens, referring to exchange in Europe between the thirteenth and seventeenth centuries:

> [Credit] threaded through the economy from the large purchases of international merchants to the survival purchases of the urban poor. Consumers did not pay for their bread, or candles, or shoes, or meat. They ran tabs with the shopkeepers. Cloth traders bought wool on credit, had it worked into cloth by weavers on credit, then sold it at the international fairs and urban entrepot towns on credit. Vintners bought wine on credit and sold it to tavernkeepers on credit. Individuals secured services from barbers, apothecaries, and wet nurses on credit. [...]
> Pre-modern commerce revolved around credit, and likely no one was spared the need to be debtor and creditor.
> Kadens (2015, pp. 2431–2432)

Thus economic exchange revolved around the creation and elimination of debts, but I must emphasize that these debts were *not* a form of money: in most cases, you could not take an existing debt, established following a transaction between two agents, and offer it as means of payment to a third party. That's what sets aside these debts from modern forms of money which, as we have seen previously, are also debts. Modern bank deposits are debts accepted by all and everyone, no questions asked. The use of bilateral debts for carrying out exchange presupposes the existence of a social relationship between the two parties involved.

---

[3] See, inter alia, von Reden (2010, p. 93), Harris (2008, p. 191), Goetzmann (2016, p. 100), and van de Mieroop (2002, p. 166).

[4] Muldrew (1998, p. 100).

Of course, payments on the spot were also required on some occasions—in particular, when either the seller or the buyer was a person not residing permanently in the local economy. In these cases, and in the words of assyriologist A. Bongenaar, "every commodity served the purpose" (Bongenaar, 1999, p. 162)—meaning, you could pay with whatever was acceptable to the seller. This comes to resemble barter, but with the important difference that all prices were defined in advance, and expressed in terms of the unit of account.

To summarize, the history of money begins with the establishment of a unit of account based on the value of some well-known or prestigious commodity. No universal means of payment is in place at this initial stage, with people using anything acceptable by their counterparty when it came to making payments on the spot. Spot payments, however, were relatively infrequent as a method to carry out exchange. Most economic exchange was carried out by establishing bilateral debts which could be cancelled out against each other at a later stage.

~~~

Ancient societies typically converge on the use of precious metals, in particular gold and silver, as the basis for their unit of account. Precious metals had an advantage over agricultural products in being far more acceptable when offered as a means of payment: they were easy to store, did not degrade over time, and had a high value per unit of weight. On the other hand, they were relatively rare and thus often unavailable, and their high value made them impractical for small payments. Thus, most of everyday exchange continued to be carried out using bilateral debts, while gold and silver in bullion form were often employed in large commercial transactions. Such was the state of affairs in the ancient world towards the end of the seventh century BC, when the history of money enters into a wholly new chapter with the invention of coinage—an object to which the word "money" can, for the first time, be attached without hesitation.

Coinage first appears in the historical record around the year 620 BC in Lydia, a kingdom of western Anatolia neighbouring the ancient Greek cities of Ephesus and Miletus.[5] Upon coming in contact with it, Greek city-states become the first societies to adopt coinage as a universal means of payment, their usage becoming increasingly common over the sixth century BC. Trade and conquest spread the use of coinage throughout

---

[5] Schaps (2004, p. 95).

the eastern Mediterranean and the Middle East, before Rome takes over as the dominant political power in the West and makes its coinage circulate from Britain to Mesopotamia. Over the following two millennia, coins never cease to be conceived as the embodiment of money.

To a certain line of thought, the invention of coinage represents only a minor improvement over the previously existing monetary system where the value of precious metals served as a unit of account and precious metal in bullion form circulated as a means of payment. Producing silver coins appears to be only a method for "packing" silver into standardized units, units which are convenient to use and with a certified quantity of metal in them. A well-accepted theory about the introduction of coinage supports this idea, advancing that coins were invented to facilitate transactions made by the state—in particular, the payment of wages for soldiers and mercenaries. Instead of weighting precious metal for the payment of every single soldier on pay day, it would have been convenient to prepare standardized pieces of metal in advance, placing the king's seal on them as a guarantee of their weight and purity.

And indeed, archeological evidence comes in support of this view of coinage in the form of coin hoards (bundles of coins hidden by their owner in ancient times, and found in modern times). The very earliest coin hoards, dating to the sixth century BC, contain a combination of coins and metal in bullion form—exactly what you would expect if both were used interchangeably as means of payment.[6] Coins, in other words, were valued as simple pieces of precious metal in the first decades following their invention.

But the archaeological record also reveals something far more interesting. Coin hoards dating to just a few generations after the earliest ones contain only coins—metal in bullion form was no longer accepted as a means of payment, and this pattern continues all the way to present times. This concurs with the historical evidence, showing that coinage was the only form of payment universally accepted by the state and in commercial transactions. When this happens, the nature of the monetary system changes in a radical way: coins cannot be say to be valued as mere pieces of precious metal if precious metal itself is not a substitute for it.

In the new monetary system that emerged, the state manufactures coins which it declares have a value in terms of a certain unit. Coins in

---

[6] Von Reden (2010, pp. 21–22).

ancient Greece, for instance, had values which were multiples or fractions of a unit called the *drachma*. Goods and services in the economy are priced in terms of this unit—in other words, the units in which the value of coins is expressed is also the unit of account in the economy. The *drachma* is therefore a quantity of economic value and can be used to measure the value of all things, but it is not defined in relation to a quantity of precious metal. The state cannot set the prices of goods and services in terms of this unit (in other words, it cannot set the value of the *drachma*). The prices of goods and services are determined according to market forces—in particular, according to the quantity of coins which the state chooses to put in circulation.

The system is confusing because the coins produced do contain precious metal, and have therefore an intrinsic value as objects, separate from the value declared by the state. The value of coins as metallic objects will not be higher than the value declared by the state, or else the coins would be melted for the metal in them. On the other hand, it is perfectly possible for coins whose intrinsic value as objects is below the value declared by the state to circulate and be accepted at this higher value, provided the public trusts this practice to prevail.

During the two thousand years following their invention, coins have typically circulated for a value which exceeds the value of the metal in them but, crucially, not by much. To take a specific example, historian and legal scholar Christine Desan tells us that this difference was "almost always less than 10 percent, and generally less than 5 percent" in England during the Late Middle Ages.[7] Indeed, through most of history people have regarded coinage whose intrinsic value falls far below its declared value with mistrust—and for good reason. The declared value is a social construction which can cease to apply, in which case the coins in question would revert to their value as objects. People will not risk seeing much of their wealth evaporate if such eventuality comes to pass. The state had to comply with the wishes of the public, or else see its currency being discarded in favour of other means of payment. This arrangement meant that the public got a form of money it could trust, while the state

---

[7] Desan (2014, p. 101).

got to collect a tidy income from the modest, but nevertheless positive, difference between the value of coins and the value of the metal in them.

At certain times and places, however, the arrangement just described could be suspended. In times of urgent need—like wars and foreign invasions—states would resort to currency debasement as a method for collecting additional revenue. Currency debasement was the issuing of coins with the same name and same declared value as currently existing ones, but with a lower metallic content. The state would receive taxes in old coins and pay for public expenditures in new, lighter coins; or would order all subjects to bring their old coins to the mint and render them the new coins. While legitimate in the case of a national emergency, the operation could be abused in the hands of an unscrupulous monarch. Between the years 1542 and 1551, for instance, King Henry VIII of England reduced the silver content of the pound by a whopping 83%—an episode known to monetary historians as "The Great Debasement".[8]

The most extreme form of currency debasement, however, consists in issuing coinage with no intrinsic value whatsoever—coinage made entirely of base metals such as copper or lead, or even cheap materials such as leather. Possibly the earliest of such episodes is also one of the most famous, taking place during the final years of the Peloponnesian war (431–404 BC), when the Greek city-states of Athens and Sparta fought each other for supremacy. Having lost its famous silver mines at Laurion to the Spartans, Athens issued an emergency coinage of bronze with a thin silver coating. The coin was essentially worthless, and was to be accepted at the same value as the famous Athenian drachmas of pure silver. Perhaps surprisingly, the Athenian public accepted the coins and Athens was able to continue the war—as it turns out, not for long. Writing a few months later, the celebrated greek playwright Aristophanes wittily refers to the episode in his comedy *The Frogs*:

> The noble silver drachma, that of old
> We were so proud of, and the recent gold,
> Coins that rang true, clean stamped and worth their weight
> Throughout the world, have ceased to circulate.
> Instead the purses of Athenian shoppers

---

[8] Rolnick et al. (1996, p. 793).

Are full of shoddy silver-plated coppers.
Just so, when men are needed by the nation,
The best have been withdrawn from circulation.[9]

I recount the episode not just for the pleasure of quoting the above passage. The use of coinage with no intrinsic value clearly had an effect on the inquisitive Greek mind. The idea that such coinage could take the place of precious metal coins permanently, rather than as an emergency measure, surfaces in all clarity a few years later in the works of one of the most influential thinkers of the time (and, indeed, of all time): Plato.

In the *Laws*, Plato advances that coinage for the purpose of internal exchange, i.e. within the confines of the state, should be made of a worthless material. Gold and silver coinage would still be required for trade with foreign lands. And in the *Republic*, Plato mentions that the ideal state would organize exchange by means of a *symbolon*—the Greek word for "symbol" which, in English translations of Plato's work, is usually rendered in this context as a "money token".[10] Plato understood that as long as the public was willing to accept money tokens for the value dictated by the state, the actual material from which the tokens were made of was irrelevant. A rational organization of society would save the expensive gold and silver for where they are really needed, and manufacture money tokens out of cheap materials.

Thus, the idea that money with no intrinsic value can become the permanent form of money in a society was present in Western thought right from its very beginnings. Over the next twenty centuries, however, the idea was essentially a road not taken. Nothing resembling Plato's money tokens gained widespread acceptance, at any rate in the West, save for short and extreme episodes related to war. People wanted solid money they could trust and, by and large, that is what they got. Money with no intrinsic value was eventually developed, but following a

---

[9] Cited in von Reden (1995, p. 114). "The recent gold" refers to coinage made out of this metal, produced by Athens in addition to its traditional silver coins. The beautiful English translation is due to David Barrett.

[10] Plato, *Laws*, book V, 742a, and *Republic*, book II, 371b.

very different route from the one first imagined by Plato. It was a route whose exploration required the agency not only of the state, but of a different type of economic entity yet to be fully developed. The forms of money which came to dominate our economic life were the creation of the modern bank.

CHAPTER 4

Banks Enter the Scene

Keywords Ancient banking · Deposit taking

The first fully specialized banks in history appear in ancient Greece towards the end of the fifth century BC—only a few decades after the widespread adoption of coins as the foremost form of money in Greek society. Before this period, we can find several banking functions being provided at different times and places by large merchants and by certain institutions, with the earliest examples going all the way back to the middle of the 3rd millennium BC in ancient Mesopotamia. The Greek case is different in that no merchant or institution before that time had made banking services their sole or main line of business. The best evidence for this is that no society before classical Greece had a word for the profession of "banker". As individuals came to fully specialize in the provision of banking services, Greek society began to refer to them as *trapezitis*—derived from *trapeza*, the Greek word for table or bench, and meaning a person who does his business behind such implement.

The appearance of banking shortly after the adoption of coinage is no coincidence, for the relationship between the two is quite marked. Banking seems to follow coinage, and does so repeatedly throughout European history. Banking is adopted by the Romans from the Greeks,

© The Author(s), under exclusive license to Springer Nature Switzerland AG 2022
L. Angeles, *Money Matters*,
https://doi.org/10.1007/978-3-030-95516-8_4

just as they adopt coinage, and made to handle larger sums than ever before. Following the fall of the Roman empire, and the accompanying economic dislocation, coinage production falls to a minimal level and coins become scarce—even ceasing to circulate altogether in the most peripheral areas of the former empire, such as Britain. When coins become scarce, banking disappears: no banks are active in Western Europe from the sixth century AD onwards.[1] By the twelfth century, however, commerce and economic activity had regained much of the vitality seen at the height of the empire and coinage production had resumed strongly. And, together with coinage and commerce, banking appears once again on the scene: the earliest evidence of dedicated banking institutions since Roman times comes from the Italian city of Genoa around the year 1150.[2] From there, banking springs back to life in commercial cities all around Mediterranean Europe during the thirteenth century (Florence, Venice, Sicily, Naples, Barcelona, Valencia) and, by the turn of the fourteenth century, also in Northern Europe (Nuremberg, Bruges, Ghent). As was the case in ancient times, the name given to these new providers of financial services is derived from the table or bench where their operations were carried out: *banchiere* in italian, from which we derive the modern words *banca* (italian), *banco* (spanish), *banque* (french) and, of course, *bank* (english and german).

Banking begins with the practice of deposit taking. The reason why banks first appear following the widespread adoption of coinage is very likely related to the fact that precious metal coins present some substantial inconveniences: they can be easily stolen, and carrying large quantities of them is impractical and risky. As soon as coinage becomes abundant, merchants and other market participants would find it convenient to have large quantities of coins deposited with a specialized agent or an official institution—especially one with dedicated and secure storage facilities. Both in ancient Greece and in late medieval Italy the profession of banker evolves from that of money changers—people in the business of exchanging the coinage of one realm for that of another one. Money changers invested in the capacity to store coins safely for their own purposes, and were ready to rent such services to others against payment.

---

[1] Bogaert et al. (1994, p. 71).

[2] Bogaert et al. (1994, p. 84).

Depositing coins with a banker became increasingly attractive as bankers offered payment services from these deposits. Instead of withdrawing coins from an existing deposit whenever making a payment, merchants would find it convenient to instruct their bank to pay a named individual on their behalf. In ancient Greece such orders of payment had to be made in person, but written orders of payment are adopted soon enough—the earliest extant examples date to the third century BC and come from Hellenistic Egypt.[3] Written orders of payment could be sent from another city or country—a very useful service for merchants, who may find themselves abroad for several months at a time. By the first century BC, such written orders of payment had been standardized and simplified enough for present-day financial historians to refer to them as the earliest examples of cheques.

Eventually, when banking becomes widespread in a city and most local merchants have an account with one of the local banks, an important transition occurs. Instead of receiving payment in the form of precious metal coinage, merchants began to accept—and eventually prefer—payment in the form of a credit to a bank deposit in their name. Just as is the case in modern times, an order of payment would then give rise to a debit on the bank deposit of the paying party and a credit on the bank deposit of the party being paid—saving people the time and hassle of dealing with coinage. The earliest evidence of the existence of this payment mechanism dates from the second century BC and comes, once again, from Hellenistic Egypt. The document is a papyrus where one finds, in the genitive, the names of people whose account had been credited and, in the dative, the names of people whose accounts had been debited. Names in the dative are indented by one centimeter to the right, to distinguish between types of transactions.[4] When this operation becomes possible, bank deposits may be called a form of money - payments could be made with them, without the intervention of coinage.

But deposit taking and the offering of payment services is only one half of the banking business—the other half being lending. Lending money has of course been part and parcel of every commercial society since times immemorial, but its existence has not implied the existence of banking. Banks differ from merchants and other market participants engaged in

---

[3] Bogaert et al. (1994, p. 27).

[4] Bogaert et al. (1994, p. 28).

money lending in the source of the money they lend and in making lending their main line of business.

It is quite likely that early bankers first engaged in the business of lending money using their own funds. As their deposit-taking activities took off, however, bankers quickly realized that most of the funds deposited with them would remain under their custody for a rather long time. Bank clients preferred to leave their coinage at banks and use bank deposits as a means of payment whenever possible. The coins received in deposit by banks were, so to say, idle. Banks learned they could safely loan out much of the coinage received to third parties, profit from the operation by charging an interest, and still satisfy requirements for coinage withdrawals from their depositors. As long as they kept a sufficient share of the coins received in their vaults, typical requests from depositors could be met with confidence.

The benefits of this activity were substantial since banks did not have to share the interest received on their loans with their depositors. In time, banking came to be defined as the business of collecting money from the public, and using this money to make loans to borrowers on the bank's behalf.

All of the above developments typically take place within a short period of time wherever banking starts to operate, and could already be witnessed in Hellenistic Egypt and ancient Rome. An important consequence of the appearance of such a business model was the evolution of a legal framework that recognized the de facto nature of the bank deposit. If banks were loaning out the coins they received for their own profit, they were not acting as mere custodians of these coins—as they would have been supposed to do under a standard deposit contract. Accordingly, jurists from ancient Rome develop the notion of the *depositum irregulare* ("irregular deposit"), which applied to deposits of coinage with banks, and which differed from the traditional notion of the *depositum regulare* ("regular deposit"), which applied to deposits of valuable items in general. With a *depositum irregulare*, the bank was required to render coins of equal value to the depositor upon demand—but not the same coins initially deposited, as would be the case with a regular deposit. If you think about it for a second, this changes the legal nature of the bank deposit from a certificate of coins held in custody to a debt, albeit the letter of the law was never perfectly clear on this point.[5]

Because of this ambiguity, the fact that bank deposits are effectively debts continues to be debated and challenged in European courts of law over the next two thousand years. It has never been easy to accept that, following deposit at a bank, the ownership of coins is transferred from the depositor to the bank. Roman law was not helpful in calling the operation a special type of deposit, rather than the establishment of a debt.

Legal disputations continued until the fairly recent past, but have since been settled. For common law countries, the nature of the bank deposit as a form of debt was decided once and for all in 1848 with a ruling by the House of Lords of the United Kingdom, then the highest court of the realm.[6] The ruling lays out how the act of depositing currency at a bank is to be understood in legal terms:

> Money, when paid into a bank, ceases altogether to be the money of the principal [i.e. the depositor] ... ; it is then the money of the banker, who is bound to return an equivalent by paying a similar sum to that deposited with him when he is asked for it.
>
> [..]
>
> ... the banker is not an agent or factor, but he is a debtor.
>
> Foley v. Hill (1848) 2 HLC 28

To summarize, the first stage of development in the business of banking consists in the establishment of institutions that take deposits of currency from the public and issue a debt in return, use at least some of the currency received to make loans on their own behalf, and offer payment services to their depositors—payments which may be carried out using currency or, alternatively, using bank deposits as a means of payment. Once this business model is in place, we may correctly say that banking expands the quantity of money in the economy—in a very meaningful sense, banks start to create money. That such is the case should not be immediately obvious to the uninitiated because these banks are

---

[5] See Geva (2011, pp. 195 and 596).

[6] Geva (2011, p. 368).

only issuing bank deposits when they take currency from the public—in other words, they increase the quantity of bank deposits available only by decreasing the quantity of currency in circulation by the same amount. This, however, does not take into account the fact that some of the currency received is put back into circulation by the process of bank lending—as I explain in what follows.

~~~

Let us imagine an ancient economy with no banks, where all money in circulation takes the form of precious metal coinage. The coinage was produced by a central government, and was put in circulation when this government used the coins produced to buy goods and services from the public. Once the coins are in the hands of the public, people use them to buy goods and services from each other—thus facilitating economic activity. To fix our ideas, let us say that all coins introduced in the economy by this method are worth 10 million drachmas—the drachma being the unit of account in which the value of all coins is expressed.

Consider now what happens when banks start to operate in this economy. Let us say the public decides to deposit half of all their currency with the banks, for a value of 5 million drachmas. Initially, this coinage will lie idle within the storage facilities of banks—unable to be used as means of payment by the public. Upon reception of the coinage, the banks will issue bank deposits for a value of 5 million drachmas, a new form of means of payment previously unavailable in the economy. The money supply of the economy thus remains equal to 10 million drachmas, now half of this in the form of coins in circulation and the other half in the form of bank deposits.

Next, banks loan out much of the funds received—let us say they use 80% of the coinage deposited for this purpose, for a value of 4 million drachmas, and keep the remainder in vault. The loans are made by physically handing coinage to borrowers, who bring them back into circulation as they use them to purchase goods and services. Following this second operation, the value of all coins in circulation increases to 9 million drachmas while the value of bank deposits remains equal to 5 million. The money supply of the economy has therefore expanded: from an initial 10 million drachmas in coins, to a final 14 million drachmas in coins and bank deposits—with 1 million in coins held out of circulation within banks' vaults. In this way, the business of banking has brought substantial benefits to society. It has made possible the expansion of the means of payment at the disposal of the public by a value of 4 million drachmas, and has done so without employing an ounce of precious metal. In addition, it has made possible the financing of borrowers for this same amount. If borrowers go on to make a productive use of the funds received, society benefits even more.

This, then, was the business of banking as practised in Antiquity and, depending on the time and place, in Europe during the Late Middle Ages. But two important observations are necessary. First and foremost, the method of money creation just described, working through the reception and transfer of currency initially held by the public, does not exist in present times. The method presupposes that the public first obtains currency directly from the state—as was indeed the case in ancient times. As we have seen in Chapter 2, however, this channel for putting currency into circulation is no longer in operation. Today, the public can only access additional currency by withdrawal from an already existing bank deposit. When the public deposits such currency back into the banking system, it is only redressing the situation that existed before the currency was withdrawn. Present-day banks create money, but they don't do it through the process described in this chapter.

Which leads me to the second observation. University courses in economics typically describe the process of money creation by banks *in present times* using the logic outlined in this chapter. Readers with an economics formation will have recognized the discussion above as the first stage of what is universally referred within the discipline as the "money multiplier" mechanism—a staple of introductory courses in economics the world over. The full money multiplier mechanism follows from the observation that some of the coinage put back into circulation via bank lending will eventually be deposited back into the banking system, generating a second round of expansion in the money supply; and the process would repeat itself ad infinitum (each time generating smaller and smaller monetary expansions). A standard exercise in introductory economics is to calculate the total amount of money created once the process has run its course.

My message here is simple. The money multiplier mechanism could be of some value if our subject of study is the economies of the ancient world (although, in that case, it is doubtful that banks would have been large enough to make much of a difference). As a guide to money creation in present-day economies, however, the money multiplier mechanism is profoundly misleading—it leads students into thinking about banks as institutions that receive currency from the public, then transfer that currency to borrowers when making loans. As I shall make clear in subsequent chapters, that business model of banking has not been current for several centuries now. The reliance of economic educators on the money multiplier mechanism to explain money creation by banks in present times cannot be abandoned soon enough.

What this chapter has described, then, is what we may refer to as *ancient banking*—a business model practiced in ancient Greece and Rome, and upon banks' reappearance during the European Middle Ages. From there onwards, banks continue to evolve and quickly transcend this business model. How this evolution took place, and where it led to, will be addressed over the next few chapters.

CHAPTER 5

The Dawn of Modern Banking

Keywords Modern banking · Deposit creation

When banks regain the scene in Western Europe during the twelfth century AD, their business model was in all fundamental aspects similar to that of ancient Roman or Greek banks. At some point during the late Middle Ages, however, banks develop a new trick which sets them aside from their predecessors in the ancient world and firmly on their way towards modern banking institutions. In short, banks invented a mechanism for creating money in the form of bank deposits without the direct intervention of currency. At its core, this is the very same mechanism that banks use to create money in the present day.

To understand how it works, let us consider an example. Imagine first a bank that begins operations and receives currency deposits for a value of £100,000. The bank issues a debt against this currency which we call a bank deposit and, initially, holds the currency in its vault. As soon as it is convenient, the bank will seek to use the currency to make loans since, as it stands, the bank is only losing money: currency pays no interest, whereas bank deposits are costly to maintain and may well be due some small interest payment. Thus, the bank will seek to loan out a large fraction of the currency received—let us say 80% of the total,

© The Author(s), under exclusive license to Springer Nature
Switzerland AG 2022
L. Angeles, *Money Matters*,
https://doi.org/10.1007/978-3-030-95516-8_5

Fig. 5.1 Bank lending
by currency transfer

Panel (a): Balance sheet after reception of currency

Bank A

Bank Assets	Bank Liabilities
Currency £100,000	Bank deposit £100,000

Panel (b): Balance sheet after lending currency to borrowers

Bank A

Bank Assets	Bank Liabilities
Currency £20,000	Bank deposit £100,000
Bank Loan £80,000	

or £80,000—while keeping the rest in vault to satisfy withdrawals. The interest income on the money loaned out will be sufficient to pay for the bank's costs and leave a profit.

Figure 5.1 shows the accounting entries which correspond to this business model—what we have referred to as ancient banking. The figure reports the balance sheet of a banking institution, unimaginatively named "Bank A". A balance sheet is an accounting device which lists all assets belonging to the bank in its left-hand side and all liabilities owed by the bank in its right-hand side. According to the principles of double-entry book-keeping, total assets and total liabilities will always match each other—an increase in one side of the balance sheet must always be matched either by an increase of equal magnitude on the other side or by a decrease of equal magnitude on the same side.

Panel (a) of Fig. 5.1 reports the balance sheet when the bank receives currency on deposit. The currency received constitutes a new asset for the bank which is added to the assets side. At the same time, the bank issues a new liability for the same value of the currency received which is added to the liabilities side and which we call a bank deposit.

In panel (b) the bank loans out currency for a value of £80,000, which leads to a change in the composition of its assets. First, currency held in vault falls to a value of £20,000. At the same time, the bank gains a new asset: a debt issued by the borrower in favour of the bank, for a value of £80,000, which we call a bank loan. The total value of assets does not change and remains in line with total liabilities. The bank has made a loan by transferring currency from depositors to borrowers.

So far, so straightforward—but let's move on. Assume now that, upon reception of currency for a value of £100,000, a borrower approaches the bank and asks for a loan of large magnitude—let us say £400,000. What a tempting prospect for the bank! If the loan was possible, interest income would be five times larger than with the loan of £80,000 considered above. Profits would grow in equal measure. The bank would dearly like to make the loan but, of course, that is impossible. The bank has no more than £100,000 worth of currency in vault, and surely it cannot lend money which it does not have. Or can it?

Consider that the events above take place in a society where bank deposits are a widely accepted means of payment—a society where bank deposits are, for all intent and purposes, a form of money. The bank may then respond to its prospective borrower that such a large loan can indeed be granted, provided it is disbursed in the form of a bank deposit (that is to say, by crediting a bank deposit in the name of the borrower with the sum of £400,000). Let us assume the borrower is satisfied with this proposal.

Where, however, will the bank get the additional bank deposit to carry out this operation? The answer is that the bank will simply issue the new bank deposit needed—it will create a bank deposit without currency being deposited. The bank can do this because a bank deposit is a debt, not a certificate for currency received. Debts may be issued by any individual or any institution at will—a debt is just a record establishing that somebody owes somebody else a given quantity of economic value. The bank is therefore free to establish a new debt against itself and in favour of the borrower, and that debt may take the form of a bank deposit.

The operation is illustrated in Fig. 5.2, once again by showing the changes on the bank's balance sheet as this mechanism is made to work. Panel (a) of this figure is identical to panel (a) of Fig. 5.1, and reports the balance sheet of the bank following the reception of currency for a value of £100,000. In panel (b), the bank approves a new loan for a value of £400,000 and proceeds to disburse the loan using bank deposits. It issues a new bank deposit for this value in the name of the borrower, which now appears on the liabilities side of the balance sheet (as "Bank deposit of borrower"). At the same time, the bank receives a new asset for this same value in the form of the loan agreed—a debt against the borrower,

Fig. 5.2 Bank lending
via bank deposit creation

Panel (a): Balance sheet after reception of currency

Bank A

Bank Assets	BankLiabilities
Currency £100,000	Bank deposit £100,000

Panel (b): Balance sheet after lending via bank deposit creation

Bank A

Bank Assets	Bank Liabilities
Currency £100,000	Bank deposit £100,000
Bank Loan £400,000	Bank deposit of borrower £400,000

an asset for the bank. The two sides of the bank's balance sheet expand by the same amount, and the equality between total assets and liabilities is maintained. I will refer to this method of bank lending as lending by bank deposit creation or, since bank deposits are money, lending by money creation.

Up to this point, lending by bank deposit creation appears to be undeniably better for the bank: on the basis of the same amount of currency received, the bank is able to generate five times the quantity of lending business. But we must not reason with haste. In Fig. 5.1, the business of lending is completed once currency is handed out to the borrower. The subsequent spending of that currency will not involve the bank in any way. In Fig. 5.2, on the other hand, business is far from over when the borrower receives a bank deposit in his name. The borrower will proceed to use this bank deposit to make payments and, unlike currency, the spending of bank deposits will require the involvement of the bank who issued the deposits in question. Our analysis of bank lending via money creation is therefore far from over.

A payment using bank deposits typically involves four parties: a buyer, a seller, the buyer's bank, and the seller's bank. In some occasions the buyer's bank is also the seller's bank, which facilitates matters, but we shall occupy ourselves only with the general case. In the general case, the seller of goods and services is accepting payment in the form of a credit to a bank deposit at her bank. In order to make this possible, the buyer's bank must put in place the following set of operations. First, it debits the buyer's bank deposit by the amount of the payment. Second, it asks the bank of the seller to credit the seller's bank deposit by the same amount—the seller's bank is thus increasing its debt towards one of its clients. Third, in order to compensate the seller's bank for this action, the buyer's bank issues a new liability against itself and in favour of the bank of the seller. This last liability would be payable on demand in the form of currency, since those are the characteristics of the bank deposit which the seller's bank has been asked to credit.

The set of operations just described is represented in Fig. 5.3. A second bank appears in this figure: "Bank B", the bank of the person who sells goods or services to the borrower of Bank A. Panels (a) and (b) of this figure are identical to the same panels in Fig. 5.2: they show the balance sheet of Bank A following a deposit of currency and the granting of a loan via bank deposit creation. Panel (c) is where we should focus our attention.

Panel (c) reports the balance sheets of both banks following the purchase of goods and services using the bank deposit created by Bank A. Bank A has debited the deposit of the borrower by £400,000—leaving a balance of zero on this account. At the same time, Bank A has issued a new debt worth £400,000 in favour of Bank B, which now appears on the liabilities side of its balance sheet. Moving on to Bank B, we observe an increase in the bank deposit of the seller of goods and services—a client of Bank B—for a value of £400,000. As we have indicated, Bank A has compensated Bank B by issuing a debt for this same amount - already visible in Bank A's balance sheet. All debts, however, appear twice in accounting documents: as a liability on the balance sheet of the debtor and as an asset on the balance sheet of the creditor. Accordingly, the debt issued by Bank A will also appear as an asset on the balance sheet of Bank B—thus equilibrating the expansion in Bank B's liabilities.[1]

---

[1] The reader should note that, in many instances of present-day bank lending, banks pass from panel (a) to panel (c) directly. In other words, loan proceeds are not disbursed to the borrower. Instead, the borrower declares in advance the intended use of the funds, and the bank disburses directly to the beneficiary. This is the case of all mortgage lending: the bank pays the loan proceeds directly to the seller of the property, while

Panel (a): Balance sheet after reception of currency

Bank A

Bank Assets	Bank Liabilities
Currency £100,000	Bank deposit £100,000

Panel (b): Balance sheet after lending via bank deposit creation

Bank A

Bank Assets	Bank Liabilities
Currency £100,000	Bank deposit £100,000
Bank loan £400,000	Bank deposit of borrower £400,000

Panel (c): Balance sheets after borrower spends the bank deposit created

Bank A

Bank Assets	Bank Liabilities
Currency £100,000	Bank deposit £100,000
Bank loan £400,000	Bank deposit of borrower £0
	Debt from Bank A to Bank B £400,000

Bank B

Bank Assets	Bank Liabilities
Debt from Bank A to Bank B £400,000	Bank deposit of seller £400,000

Fig. 5.3 Bank lending and spending of bank deposit

At this point, Bank A finds itself in a tricky position. It has issued a debt in favour of another bank which is payable on demand. Bank B has no reason to delay requesting payment of this debt—particularly when additional currency may come handy for its own business plans. With nothing else changing in the economic environment, Bank B will ask for immediate payment of this debt in currency form. If that is the case, lending by bank deposit creation would give rise to a currency outflow towards other

the borrower gains ownership of the property in question. The same is true for credit card debt.

banks for the full amount of the loan. This has often led economists to claim that lending by bank deposit creation is not different from lending by currency transfer. In both cases, the lending bank would need to have currency available for the full amount of the loan—only the timing of the currency outflow would differ, which would be a matter of minor importance.

This view, however, is mistaken. The above scenario counterfactually assumes that only one bank in the economy is engaged in bank deposit creation—Bank A in our example. In an economy with multiple banks, however, that will never be the case: all banks engage in lending by bank deposit creation at the same time. This changes our conclusions radically, as every bank will become not only a debtor but also a creditor to the other banks in the system. The business of banking cannot be understood by considering one bank in isolation—we must look at the banking sector as a whole.

To illustrate the point, let us think of an economy with two banks—Bank A and Bank B—where both banks engage simultaneously in lending via bank deposit creation. As before, we shall assume that bank borrowers need to pay a seller of goods and services who holds a bank account with the other bank in the system—Bank B represents the rest of the banking system for Bank A, and viceversa. The final panel of Fig. 5.3 has described the balance sheets of Banks A and B when Bank A does the lending. Figure 5.4, then, starts by reproducing this situation and adds the entries that correspond to lending by Bank B. Lending by Bank B produces entries which are the mirror image of those produced by the lending of Bank A.

In panel (a) of Fig. 5.4, Bank A owes bank deposits for a value of £500,000. This corresponds to the initial deposit of £100,000 issued upon reception of currency, plus the £400,000 credited to the bank deposit of one of its clients by request of Bank B. Bank A had also credited and subsequently debited £400,000 to the bank deposit of its borrower, but this is no longer visible. On the assets side, we find the £100,000 worth of currency received plus the loan made for a value of £400,000. In addition to this, Bank A has a debt in favour of Bank B for a value of £400,000, and holds a claim against Bank B for this same value. The same entries appear, mutatis mutandis, in the balance sheet of Bank B.

At this point, instead of claiming payment of the debts held against each other, the two banks will simply agree to cancel them. The debt of Bank A towards Bank B for a value of £400,000 will be cancelled against

Panel (a): Balance sheets after lending via bank deposit creation and after borrowers spend their loans

Bank A		**Bank B**	
Bank Assets	*Bank Liabilities*	*Bank Assets*	*Bank Liabilities*
Currency £100,000	Bank deposits £500,000	Currency £100,000	Bank deposits £500,000
Bank loan £400,000		Bank loan £400,000	
Debt from Bank B to Bank A £400,000	Debt from Bank A to Bank B £400,000	Debt from Bank A to Bank B £400,000	Debt from Bank B to Bank A £400,000

Panel (b): Balance sheets after banks cancel out each other's debts

Bank A		**Bank B**	
Bank Assets	*Bank Liabilities*	*Bank Assets*	*Bank Liabilities*
Currency £100,000	Bank deposits £500,000	Currency £100,000	Bank deposits £500,000
Bank loan £400,000		Bank loan £400,000	

Fig. 5.4 Bank lending at the aggregate level

the debt of Bank B towards Bank A for that same amount. The resulting balance sheets are shown in panel (b) of Fig. 5.4, which is the final stage of the process of bank lending when analysed at the level of the banking sector as a whole. At this point, banks have created bank deposits for a value of £400,000 each, borrowers have gone on to use these bank deposits for the purchase of goods and services, and no currency movements between banks have taken place as a consequence. Banks have succeeded in making loans which far exceed the amount of currency they hold in reserve—something that would have been impossible when lending via currency transfer.

A very similar logic will apply in an economy with more than two banks. Each bank in the system becomes indebted to all other banks for the quantity of bank deposits it creates but, at the same time, becomes a creditor to other banks in proportion to the bank deposits that they create. As long as the debtor positions resulting from this activity are cancelled out by the creditor positions, the banks will not see an outflow of currency. Banks will be creating money in the form of bank deposits through the process of bank lending, and this money creation will not be constrained by their holdings of currency. John Maynard Keynes, possibly the most influential economist of the twentieth century, understood well this logic when he advanced, back in the year 1930, that "there is no limit to the amount of bank money [i.e. bank deposits] which the banks can safely create *provided that they move forward in step*" (Keynes 1930, p. 23; italics in the original). "Moving forward in step" means creating bank deposits in line with other banks in the system, so that the resulting debts towards other banks are neatly balanced by the resulting credits against them.

Of course, real-life banking systems will not be so perfectly coordinated. Some banks will create bank deposits in excess of their peers, resulting in a net debtor position towards the rest of the system. This, however, does not represent a problem. Net debts may be cancelled out by currency transfers—debtor banks will lose currency, but only for the difference between their gross debtor and gross creditor positions towards other banks in the system, which may be quite manageable. Alternatively, notice that the existence of net debtors logically implies the existence of net creditors: every debt between banks is a liability for one bank but an asset for another one. Thus, debtor banks may ask banks in a net credit position to lend them currency. Such loans would be payable after a certain term and, as such, would carry an interest. Interest payments would constitute a transfer of income from banks in a net debtor position to banks in a net creditor position—a penalty for those banks creating bank deposits in excess of the system.

To summarize, banks are perfectly capable of granting loans by issuing or creating new bank deposits—a method which is fundamentally different from lending by currency transfer. Lending by bank deposit creation does not lead to currency outflows for the average bank in the system—provided that all banks in the system are engaged in the practice. Thanks to this mechanism, banks are able to make loans which can be several times larger than the amount of currency they hold in reserve, as illustrated in Figs. 5.2, 5.3, and 5.4. Lending by bank deposit creation expands the size of the banking business, and therefore banking profits, several times over—which is why the practice tends to spread as soon as bank deposits are a widely accepted means of payment.

From its origins during the Late Middle Ages, the mechanism just described becomes the dominant and eventually the only way in which banks make loans to the public. Today, banks make loans only via bank deposit creation, and bank deposit creation is effectively responsible for all the expansion in the money supply we observe year after year. Currency holdings increase as well, but only as the public exchanges some of the bank deposits created into currency. The transition towards this method of money creation, however, was far from swift. It took place over a period of no less than five centuries, and required a number of additional innovations which we discuss in what follows.

CHAPTER 6

The Creation of a Paper Currency

Keywords Bank reserves · Bank run · Banknote · Public banks · Bank of England · Central Bank · Convertibility

Lending by bank deposit creation was invented during the Late Middle Ages, albeit we have no precise dating for it. In a classic article, the economic historian Abbott Parson Usher argued that the practice was probably well established by the early fifteenth century, when written sources from Venice imply its existence.[1] Subsequent work has argued for the middle of the fourteenth century as the most likely period for its appearance.[2] If so, it took banks more than five centuries to go from discovering this mechanism to turning it into the main engine of money creation in advanced economies—something that was achieved only between the late nineteenth century and the early twentieth century. At the time when the mechanism was first discovered, much had still to change for banks to uncover its full potential.

For a long time, the development of banking was held in check due to the nature of currency as precious metal coinage. As long as precious

---

[1] Usher (1934, p. 400).

[2] De Roover (1974, p. 215), Geva (2011, p. 361).

L. Angeles, *Money Matters*, https://doi.org/10.1007/978-3-030-95516-8_6

metal coins were the only form of money enjoying universal acceptance, banks could not expand their business beyond a certain size, nor make it sufficiently secure.

To understand why, we need to refer to the process of lending via bank deposit creation as described in the previous chapter. As explained there, banks can engage in this process without suffering outflows of currency to other banks. This may lead readers to think that banks can engage in deposit creation without holding any currency whatsoever, but that is not the case. Banks can avoid currency outflows to other banks, but they must still ready themselves for currency outflows towards the general public.

Once lending via bank deposit creation has been implemented, banks find themselves in the following financial position. Their assets are constituted mainly by bank loans–debts which are payable to them over a period of months or years. Their liabilities, on the hand, are mainly in the form of bank deposits—debts which the bank promises to pay at any moment on demand, by handing out currency. The public does demand payment of these liabilities—in other words, it withdraws currency from bank deposits—but, under normal circumstances, only for a fraction of their total value. Banks cannot satisfy this demand by liquidating their assets, as this would take time and probably lead to losses. Instead, banks must keep currency in vault, but only for a fraction of the value of their total bank deposits.

To give a numerical example, let us return to the case of lending via bank deposit creation from Fig. 5.4. Assume that banks have established that, in order to ensure currency withdrawals are always met, they need to keep currency for a value of 20% of bank deposits. The final panel of Fig. 5.4 then tells us that banks have reached the limit of their money-creation abilities. They have issued bank deposits for a total value of £500,000, while holding currency in vault for a value of £100,000—or 20% of deposits. Banks could decide to issue more bank deposits in order to finance more loans and increase their profits—there is no technical barrier to them doing so. In that case, however, their currency holdings would fall below the 20% mark which, by assumption, is a safety line they do not wish to cross.

In order to continue lending via bank deposit creation, then, the banks of Fig. 5.4 would need to hold additional currency. In banking parlance, they would need to increase their *bank reserves*. At a time when these reserves had to be in the form of precious metal coins, that constituted a problem: gold and silver were available in limited quantities, making coinage usually scarce. Bank development was therefore held back because bank deposit creation had to be kept in proportion to bank reserves, and bank reserves could not grow beyond the strict limits imposed by the existing quantity of coinage in circulation.

In addition to this limit on bank money creation, the use of precious metal coinage as bank reserves also made banks unsafe. Consider the financial structure of banks once again. Banks are profitable enterprises because they hold assets that are illiquid, such as bank loans, while owing liabilities that are highly liquid, such as bank deposits. Illiquid assets pay a high interest rate, whereas liquid liabilities are due a small or nil interest rate (plus the cost of providing payment services in the case of bank deposits).

This profitability, however, comes with a risk. We have mentioned above that, under normal circumstances, banks only need to keep reserves for a share of the value of bank deposits in order to satisfy currency withdrawals. Sometimes, however, circumstances are not normal. If, for whatever reason, a large number of deposit holders decides to withdraw a large fraction of their deposits at the same time, the bank will not be able to comply.

Banking would have been an easy way to make money if such eventuality never materialized but, with inevitable regularity, it did. The result is what we call a *bank run*: deposit owners quite literally run to the bank to have their deposits paid in currency, knowing that the amount of currency held by the bank is only sufficient to pay those who make this request first. When the currency runs out, the bank is effectively in default of its obligations. Bank deposits then become debts which are not convertible into currency at will and, as such, lose their widespread acceptance as means of payment—in short, they cease to be money. In the most optimist scenario, the bank may still be able to pay these debts in the future as the loans it holds reach maturity. Typically, the bank will be taken over either by another bank or by a public authority before that happens.

Why would a bank run take place? A number of good reasons may be advanced. The bank may have made loans which have not been repaid, invested in unsuccessful business ventures, or let its currency reserves fall too low. These are all instances of bank mismanagement, and will sow doubts among deposit owners about the bank's capacity to fulfil its obligations. More perversely, banks which are managed correctly and avoid the pitfalls just mentioned may also find themselves subject to bank runs. Even the suspicion of badly managed affairs—whether true or entirely fabricated—may be enough to spread the fear among a sufficient number of bank depositors and convince them to claim their money in hard currency, just in case. Thus, while bank runs have often been the outcome of a poorly managed state of affairs, it has also been the case that banks whose activities were in order—and beneficial to society—have been brought to their knees by an unexpected bank run.

This fragility of the banking business was understood by perceptive observers many centuries ago. Here, for instance, is Tommaso Contarini, Senator of the Republic of Venice during the late sixteenth century, discussing the problem with particular acuity:

> A suspicion born, a voice heard, that there is no cash or that the banker has suffered some loss, a person seen at that time withdrawing money, is enough to incite everyone to take his money and the bank, unable to meet the demand, is condemned to fail. The failure of a debtor, a disaster in some venture, the fear of war is enough to destroy this enterprise, because all creditors, fearing the loss of their money, will want to insure themselves by withdrawing it and will bring about its complete destruction. It is too difficult, indeed impossible that in the space of a few years one of these events fails to occur that bring about the ruin of the bank.
>   Cited in Roberds and Velde (2016, p. 331)

But why is this risk, inherent to the very nature of the banking business, related to the use of precious metal coinage as bank reserves? Because, as we shall see, banks can stop a nascent bank run on its track if they are capable of procuring themselves additional currency on short notice. If banks can do this, any demands for currency withdrawals above the normal state of affairs can be met with confidence—killing any rumour of bank fragility before it has the time to spread and develop. Banking can therefore become a safe business, but only if a flexible supply of bank reserves is made accessible to them. As long as bank reserves were in the form of gold and silver coinage, that was simply not possible.

By the end of the Middle Ages, it became increasingly evident that currency, in the form of precious metal coins, was holding down the financial and commercial development of European societies. Its scarcity made spot payments difficult, limited the growth of bank reserves, and made banking excessively risky. A more plentiful form of currency was badly needed, but no one could say how that could be achieved.

~~~

The development of a new form of currency came via the confluence of two financial innovations: the creation of public banks, and the invention of the banknote.

Public banks are banking institutions established with the special support of a local or national government, granted unique privileges in the conduct of their business and, in many cases, playing a leading role in the financing of the state. In exchange for this privileged position, public banks are typically subject to more restrictions than standard commercial banks—for instance, in the type of lending activity they can engage in. Albeit the literature refers to them as public banks, up until the nineteenth century many of these institutions were owned by the private sector and generated profits for their owners.

The earliest public banks were established at the beginning of the fifteenth century by the governments of some of Europe's leading commercial cities: Barcelona in the year 1401, Genoa and Valencia in 1408, Venice in 1587. The city of Amsterdam founded what became Europe's most important bank in 1609, while other influential banks were established in Hamburg (1619), Nuremberg (1621), Delft (1621) and Rotterdam (1635).[3] The Bank of Amsterdam was eventually overtaken during the eighteenth century by the Bank of England, founded in 1694. The Bank of England was only the second case of a public bank linked to a large national government—the first of its kind being Sweden's Riksbank, established in 1668. National public banks were eventually to redefine the functioning of the monetary system, but most of the transformation took place during the nineteenth century—when the Bank of England was adopted as the model to follow by nations all over Europe and, subsequently, the world.

Public banks are established from the fifteenth century onwards mainly for two reasons. First, to ensure the functioning of the payments systems. From Barcelona to Venice, transfers of bank deposits had become the most important method of payment in large commercial transactions. Bank runs would put this system in disarray by rendering the deposits of one or more banks unacceptable as a means of payment. Bank runs could cause all payments to stop, severely disrupting commerce and economic activity—something that had to be prevented at all costs.

---

[3] See Roberds and Velde (2016) for a history and taxonomy.

A public bank was therefore set up to ensure the resilience of the payments system. If the public bank could be made so secure that it would never suffer from bank runs, its deposits would always be accepted as a means of payment. To achieve this, public banks could only make loans to institutions with an unblemished financial reputation and were obliged to keep a particularly high ratio of reserves to bank deposits. In a few cases, such as Venice's Banco di Rialto, the bank may be prohibited from making loans altogether—effectively becoming a deposit holder and provider of payment services, rather than a bank. Since lending is the source of bank profits, restrictions on lending practice are accompanied by important privileges that procure the bank an income—like monopoly positions over certain banking operations. By and large, this institutional design was successful—public banks had safer asset portfolios and gained the trust of the public, making runs against them quite rare. While public banks could and did fail, their longevity was far superior to that of standard commercial banks.

What undermined the system, however, was the second reason for the establishment of public banks. Banks were a major source of financing for local economies, and the largest borrower in most economies was often the state. It was inevitable that states would seek the assistance of banks to cover fiscal deficits, and public banks were often founded with this specific purpose in mind. When the state was perceived as a responsible borrower, being the financer of the state brought reputation and a sense of security. When the opposite was the case, exposure to public debt could be the very cause of a bank run.

By the late seventeenth century, then, public banks were well established in a number of European cities and supplied banking services to the public and the state alongside commercial banking institutions. Such was the financial landscape when banknotes come into play.

A banknote is nothing other than a debt recorded on a piece of paper, issued by a bank, and payable not to a named individual but to the bearer of the note. When banknotes were first introduced in Europe during the seventeenth century, they were debts payable in precious metal coinage—the only method for cancelling debts which was accepted by everyone and everywhere. Members of the public could bring banknotes to their issuer, and be paid the amount indicated on them in lawful coins of the realm. Present-day banknotes are still formally debts, issued by the Central Bank rather than commercial banks, but no longer payable in precious metal form. I will have more to say on the subject of present-day banknotes, before the end of this chapter.

Being bank debts, banknotes have much in common with bank deposits. When depositing coins at a bank, a depositor could choose between receiving a credit to a bank deposit in his name or, alternatively, receiving banknotes. When granting loans, banks could finance borrowers by issuing bank deposits or by handing over newly printed banknotes. The interest of having banknotes instead of bank deposits was the ease of carrying out payments with them. Banknotes require no written or oral order of payment, no signatures, no witnesses, no accounting entries. We pay by handing over the banknotes to our counterparty, just as we do with coins.

Banknotes were first introduced by banking institutions in Sweden from the1660 s onwards, and the practice had been adopted in England by the late seventeenth century. These early banknotes were widely accepted among commercial circles, but they were resolutely not equal to coinage in the eyes of the public—in other words, they were not yet a form of currency. Like bank deposits, banknotes were a form of money of limited circulation—convenient to use and acceptable for many purposes, but rarely seen outside the main commercial centers and not much used by the common folk. Something needed to be added to the mix, to make banknotes universally accepted.

That something is discovered during the last years of the seventeenth century, with the creation of the Bank of England. The Bank was established in 1694 with the specific aim of providing finance to a government in desperate need of money to wage major war operations on the European continent. A number of schemes were brought to the attention of the British monarch as a means to raise money—some of them of a decidedly dubious nature. Establishing a bank which would make loans to the government appeared as a rather safe bet.

What sets the Bank of England apart from earlier experiments with public banks elsewhere in Europe is the combination of the role as main financer of the state with the practice of issuing banknotes. Public banks had existed for almost three hundred years, and banknotes had been in circulation since the middle of the seventeenth century, but the two had not been brought together previously. The Bank of England made loans to the English crown by issuing banknotes, which the English crown went on to spend in goods and services throughout the economy. This did not preclude the Bank from conducting other banking operations, including issuing its banknotes to other agents in the economy. Given the visibility and prestige of both the English crown and the newly established Bank of England, the notes were accepted well beyond their usual range of circulation.

A crucial step then befalls. Recipients of these Bank of England notes offer them back to the government when the time comes for the payment of taxes. If the state expected the public to accept the notes in payments, it seemed only natural that it would be ready to receive them in return, which it did. From the point of view of the state, accepting the notes made sense since they could be used to finance government purchases once again or, alternatively, could be handed back to the Bank of England as payment for the state's debt. A debt owed to the Bank of England can always be cancelled against a debt owed by the Bank of England, which is what Bank of England notes are.[4]

The practice made Bank of England notes the only form of money acceptable for the payment of taxes other than precious metal coinage. Somewhat unwittingly, the whole weight and prestige of the state had been recruited to lend credibility to this particular form of bank debt. Until that time, banknotes had been accepted on the basis that their issuers would exchange them for precious metal coinage on demand— a promise that could fail to materialize. Bank of England notes were different because, in addition to convertibility into precious metal, there was an implicit promise by the state that the notes would always be accept- able as a means for the payment of taxes. Something that serves to pay taxes has value, even if convertibility into metal were to fail.

It is then in Britain that a new monetary system begins to take shape. For two thousand years until then, precious metal coins had been the only form of money with the explicit backing of the state, and the only one enjoying universal circulation. From the eighteenth century onwards, Bank of England notes match them in the public's consideration. Without anyone really taking a conscious decision in the matter, the currency of the realm had been expanded by the value of such notes in circulation.

~~~

It took more than one hundred years for the British invention of banknotes issued by a privileged public bank to become popular in the European continent, and another hundred years for it to reach its logical

---

[4] See Desan (2014, Chapter 8) for a detailed description of this episode.

potential. Banknotes remain largely a British curiosity over the eighteenth century, but become increasingly common throughout Europe during the nineteenth century. Coinage was too scarce for the needs of commerce, and a system where mere paper served as a substitute was obviously attractive.

As this system gained in popularity, and banknotes came to be accepted as another form of currency alongside coinage, governments start to move in order to regulate their issuance. Up until the nineteenth century, banknotes were regularly issued by a large number of private commercial banks. Private banknotes did not enjoy the same level of acceptability as those issued by a large public bank, and their range of circulation was more limited, but they did serve the needs of commerce. On the other hand, excessive issuance of private banknotes could lead to a bank run if a sufficiently large number of note holders decided to present them for payment—the same mechanism discussed previously for the case of bank deposits. Eager to make banknotes a more reliable form of money, governments decide to intervene.

In 1844 the British government legislates to end the production of banknotes by private institutions—not immediately, but progressively over the next few decades. The goal was to render Bank of England notes the only banknotes in circulation, and to set up strict rules for their future production. Since convertibility into gold was considered of paramount importance for the notes' acceptance, the Bank of England could only produce banknotes in proportion to its reserve of precious metal.

This model is then followed by all European nations, who move to create what begins to be called a Central Bank, and give it monopoly over the production of banknotes. After Britain and Sweden in the seventeenth century, the next national public bank is the Bank of France, established by Napoleon in the year 1800. This is then followed by the Bank of Norway (1816), the Bank of Spain (1856, but preceded by other public banks), the Reichsbank in Germany (1876, but preceded by the Bank of Prussia and the public banks of numerous German states), the Bank of Japan (1882), the Bank of Italy (1893), the Swiss National Bank (1907) and, quite a latecomer, the Federal Reserve Bank of the United States in 1913. By the late nineteenth century, the doctrine that every country should have a Central Bank under government oversight and in charge of the production of banknotes was well-established in most places.

Also by the late nineteenth century, a doctrine known to history as the Gold Standard is adopted by all major economies. Under this system, the most important form of currency in all economies is the Central Bank note, which is convertible into gold at a fixed parity. The gold parities of the different currencies determine the exchange rates between them, and international trade is facilitated by the assurance that all currencies are backed up by gold, and convertible into it.

The great weakness of the system was the limited capacity of issuing banknotes, as their issuance was restricted by the gold reserves of each country's Central Bank. The introduction of banknotes made possible a larger production of currency than the previous system based exclusively on coinage, but a limit was still in place. As economies grew, their needs for ever larger quantities of money represented a problem. It is within this context that societies began to consider the idea of non-convertible banknotes.

While the idea of non-convertible banknotes appeared preposterous to some, experience had shown the concept needn't be considered outlandish. Convertibility had been suspended in several countries during major wars, and notes had continued to circulate successfully—sometimes for surprisingly long periods. The two most prominent examples were the Napoleonic wars, when Britain suspended the convertibility of Bank of England notes from 1797 until 1821, and the First World War, when all major belligerents suspended convertibility from the beginning of the war until the late 1920s. The suspension of convertibility allowed governments to produce additional banknotes in large quantities to pay for the war effort, while ensuring that a run on the Central Bank would not take place.

To be sure, supporters of the Gold Standard argued that these war episodes had been possible only because the public trusted that a return to convertibility would take place once the war would be over. They also emphasized that non-convertibility would quickly result in overproduction of banknotes, excessive inflation, and economic chaos. Returning to convertibility after a suspension episode was always a painful affair, as the amount of currency in circulation had to be brought down to a level consistent with the reserves of precious metal. As I shall discuss in the second part of this book, reducing money in circulation is a very effective method to send an economy into recession. Until the 1920s, however, conventional wisdom had it that this was a necessary effort which all responsible governments had a duty to undertake.

Eventually, reform was forced on all economies during the 1930s when a series of banking crises of sufficiently large scale arrived in the form of the Great Depression. Producing and spending large amounts of money was necessary to fight the depression, and convertibility of banknotes into gold was abandoned, this time for good.

Or almost for good. Following the Second World War, an attempt was made to revive the Gold Standard in a restricted form under what became known as the Bretton Woods system. Under this system, the currencies of all participating nations were not convertible into gold but into US dollars, which remained convertible into gold. The Bretton Woods system survived with difficulties until 1971, when the United States unilaterally decided to rescind the convertibility of the dollar—eliminating the last vestiges of a system which had guaranteed the value of currency by linking it to an object of intrinsic value.

The abandonment of convertibility into precious metal transformed banknotes into something rather unique. As has always been the case, banknotes up to the present day continue to be issued as debts owed by the Central Bank. Every Bank of England note continues to carry the legend "I promise to pay the bearer on demand the sum of [five/ten/twenty] pounds", denoting its status as a debt instrument. Notes from other countries may not declare their nature so openly, but they are all issued as debts nevertheless.

If banknotes are Central Bank debts, however, they are debts of a particular kind indeed. Banknotes had been given the status of *legal tender* before convertibility was abandoned—a status they shared alongside precious metal coinage. Legal tender is a means of payment which cannot be legally refused by a creditor for the payment of debts denominated in the unit of account. When precious metal coinage is discontinued, Central Bank notes become the only form of legal tender in circulation. What would then happen if you take a ten-pound Bank of England note, which is a debt, and present it to the Bank of England for payment? The answer is that the Bank of England would quietly accept your note and proceed to pay you using legal tender, by handing you another ten-pound note. Understandably, Central Banks will not engage in such pointless activity, which is why our modern Central Bank notes cannot be presented for payment—and may be rightfully described as token money de facto, but not de jure.

In a sense, then, economies during the twentieth century had finally developed the ideal form of currency first advanced by Plato some 23 centuries earlier. Albeit formally issued as debts, Central Bank notes may well be described as token money: they are worthless pieces of paper whose value is assigned by decree, and which people accept as payment in the knowledge that all other members of society will accept them later on, when the time comes to offer them. Their value derives from the trust people bestow on them, which is ultimately founded on the promise of the state to accept them under all circumstances in payments to itself.

CHAPTER 7

Modern Banking Comes of Age

Keywords Central Bank · Bank reserves · Convertibility · Deposit insurance · Standing facility · Interest rate policy · Open Market Operations

With the development of Central Bank notes as a new form of currency, an evolutionary process is put in motion which eventually results in a profound transformation of the business of banking. By the twentieth century, this transformation meant that the former limits to the expansion of banking could be set aside. Banks came to take the leading role in the process of money creation, and money would be created in quantities never seen before.

When Central Bank notes begin to be considered as equivalent to precious metal coins, banks proceed to use them as an alternative form of bank reserves. More bank reserves meant more bank lending, and therefore a larger banking business. This, however, was only the beginning. Keeping bank reserves in the form of coinage or Central Bank notes is costly, as they require a storage space and must be protected from the risk of theft. Since reserves are typically not needed all at once, it makes sense for all banks to store most of their reserves centrally, thus sharing

L. Angeles, *Money Matters*,
https://doi.org/10.1007/978-3-030-95516-8_7

the costs of storage and security. The institution best placed to provide this service to banks was, naturally, the newly established Central Bank.

In practice, commercial banks would deposit coins and banknotes with the Central Bank and receive a bank deposit in return. Like standard bank deposits, these "Central Bank deposits" are simply debts—they are issued by the Central Bank in favour of commercial banks, and are payable in the form of Central Bank notes or precious metal coinage on demand. Commercial banks would keep a small amount of currency in their vaults to satisfy day-to-day withdrawals from the public, and replenish this fund as needed by withdrawing from their Central Bank deposit. Bank reserves were henceforth the sum of Central Bank deposits and any currency held in vault.

The introduction of Central Bank deposits leads to a further innovation. Whenever banks need to settle debts among themselves, it will be most convenient to do so by means of Central Bank deposits. As we have seen, banks can end up in a net debtor position towards other banks as a result of lending via bank deposit creation. These net positions were traditionally cancelled out by a transfer of currency, but a far less costly and more rapid method would be the transfer of Central bank deposits from debtor banks to creditor banks. The creditor bank can then exchange these deposits for currency, if it so wishes. In this way, the Central Bank progressively takes the functions of a "bank of banks". Just like commercial banks issue regular bank deposits to members of the public and handle all payments using these deposits, the Central Bank issues Central Bank deposits to commercial banks and handles all interbank payments using them. The widespread use of Central Bank deposits as bank reserves meant the vast majority of precious metal coinage not in the hands of the public ends up being held by the Central Bank.

But the analogy of the Central Bank as a higher-level "bank of banks" does not stop there. As we have seen, commercial banks can issue bank deposits not only upon reception of currency, but against the issuance of bank loans—loans which constitute an asset for banks. Central Banks can do the same, issuing Central Bank deposits against financial assets offered by commercial banks in return. These financial assets could be newly issued debt, in which case the operation is almost identical to lending by commercial banks, or they could be assets first issued by the public or by the government, and which commercial banks have previously acquired via bank lending. This exchange of assets for Central Bank deposits steadily grows in importance, and eventually becomes the main mechanism for increasing bank reserves. Without having consciously decided to do so, the Central Bank finds itself playing a role at the very heart of the emerging monetary system: it becomes the main supplier of the country's bank reserves.

~~~

With the Central Bank assuming responsibility for the adequate supply of bank reserves, banks are finally able to break free from the constraints imposed by a metallic currency. As you may recall, banks were limited by the need to collect more and more currency in order to back up bank deposit creation, and suffered from chronic instability due to bank runs. It was the need to address bank runs which first motivates the changes that were to follow.

A bank run manifests itself as an insufficiency of bank reserves in the face of large withdrawal requirements. The logical answer to this, from the perspective of bank managers, is to procure additional reserves from wherever these may be available. If the public finds that its withdrawal requirements are being met, it may regain trust in the bank and abandon its run.

One way of implementing this idea is by borrowing reserves from other banks. The procedure can work, but is far from being fool-proof. Bank runs have a habit of coming in packs as fear is contagious. If Alpha Bank is in trouble, shouldn't that mean Beta Bank, which has made similar loans and invested in similar assets, may also be in trouble? The time when a bank run is taking place is often the worst time to go asking for reserves from other banks—they may need them for their own safety.

Not only that but, even if some banks are under no pressure and have reserves available to lend, they may well refuse them. For a start, it's risky—if the bank under pressure ends up failing, the reserves lent may be lost. And, even if a large enough support package can be arranged which guarantees the safety of the bank under pressure, why would other banks make efforts to save a competitor? Thus, help from other banks may be forthcoming if it's in those banks' own interest to do so—mainly to forestall the spread of bank runs across the system. If the bank run is not likely to spread, or if it has spread already and other banks need their reserves for themselves, no solution should be expected via this mechanism.

With the use of Central Bank deposits as bank reserves, however, a different course of action emerges. Instead of competing among themselves for a limited quantity of bank reserves in the system, banks now have the option to approach the supplier of bank reserves and ask for additional production. Unlike precious metal coinage, Central Bank deposits and banknotes can be produced at will, provided the Central Bank is ready to accept the assets that commercial banks are able to offer for them. In a word, the Central Bank is in an unmatched position to act as guardian of the stability of the financial system.

This guardianship was no mission for a privately owned profit-making institution with no particular reason to care about the health of banks in general or the repercussions of bank runs on the public—a description which fits the few national public banks in existence before the nineteenth century. The Bank of England was notoriously reticent to come to the rescue of commercial banks in trouble all along the eighteenth century, and was keen to remind financial market participants that it was under no obligation to do so.

Such an attitude would simply not do. The needs of society result in a change in the nature of Central Banking practice during the nineteenth century. From being a private institution with no specific obligations to society, the Central Bank becomes a public institution charged with a dual mandate: to ensure the convertibility of Central Bank notes into precious metal, and to safeguard the stability of the financial system at large. The acceptance of this dual mandate was achieved progressively in the British case, through legal reform and change of institutional culture. Elsewhere in Europe, and in the rest of the world afterwards, Central Banks were typically established as public institutions with this dual mandate from inception.

As the role of the Central Bank develops, a practical method for dealing with incipient financial panics and bank runs is devised in Britain during the second half of the nineteenth century, and promptly imitated elsewhere. The method was described in 1873 by Walter Bagehot, British journalist and lead editor of *The Economist* magazine, in his classic treatise *Lombard Street*. From it derives what became known as Bagehot's rule, which summarizes quite well the guiding principles a Central Bank should follow in times of financial stress. In short, a Central Bank should provide additional reserves to commercial banks when asked to do so, and should do it decisively and in any amount required. On the other hand, the Central Bank should only accept high quality assets against its reserves and should charge a discount rate which penalizes to some extent the use of this mechanism.

Bagehot's rule was followed with reasonable success during the nineteenth century, but not without highlighting a deep-seated problem. From the very beginning, it escaped nobody's attention that safeguarding the stability of banks could be in direct opposition to the Central Bank's other mandate—ensuring the convertibility of banknotes. Convertibility required that banknote production would not exceed a certain multiple of the gold reserves at the disposal of the Central Bank. This limit also applied to Central Bank deposits, as these were convertible into banknotes anyway. In other words, Central Bank notes and Central Bank deposits had to be backed by gold reserves, typically to the tune of between 35 and 50% of their value according to each country's regulations. It follows that a large financial crisis forced countries into a crossroads. In order to ensure the survival of banks, a large amount of additional Central Bank deposits and Central Bank notes had to be issued. At the same time, issuing deposits and notes in large amounts would breach the limits imposed by existing gold reserves and put convertibility at risk.

The said crossroads was surprisingly easy to reach. Britain legislated to restrict the production of banknotes by the Bank of England in 1844 and found itself facing a financial crisis that could only be dealt by suspending this restriction three years later, in 1847. The same point was reached for a second time in 1857, and for a third time in 1866. On each occasion, the Bank of England was given permission to break the law restricting its production of notes and Central Bank deposits in order to reassure the public that currency was available and banks were solvent. On each occasion, suspending the law saved Britain from major financial collapse; but having a rule that applied at all times except when it didn't was not a way to run a country.

Eventually, this somewhat haphazard approach was rendered obsolete with the abandonment by all countries of gold convertibility during the 1930s, as discussed in the preceding chapter. With no more ties to gold to protect, Central Banks could produce and lend reserves with virtually no limit—even the most widespread episode of bank runs and financial panic could in principle be repelled successfully. Not only that but, in a logic that would be familiar to war strategists, having access to unlimited financial firepower rendered its use largely unnecessary. A bank run takes place when the public believes the deposits of a given bank may not be converted into currency. If it becomes known that the institution which produces the currency is ready to support all banks, and faces no limitations in how large that support may be, there is simply no reason to start a bank run.

Indeed, once Central Banks were in a position to offer unlimited support, their policy in this area changes. Instead of offering an implicit and limited promise of financial assistance to banks, they issue an explicit and universal promise to all bank deposit owners that their money will not be lost in case of bank failure—a piece of financial legislation now present throughout the world and known as deposit insurance. Deposit insurance simply states that if a commercial bank fails to fulfill its obligations, the Central Bank will step in to pay bank deposit owners in full –albeit, typically, only up to a certain maximum amount per person. The maximum amount covered is set high enough so that the vast majority of deposit owners have nothing to fear (currently £85,000 in the United Kingdom, €100,000 in the Euro Zone, and $250,000 in the United States). With deposit insurance in place, bank runs have become largely a thing of the past.

As an example of this, consider the case of the United States. During the 1920s, a decade of optimism and rapid economic growth, the country experienced more than 600 bank failures per year—almost two bank failures per day on average. Many of these banks were small, and the country had in the region of 25,000 banks, but this is still remarkable banking instability. The number of bank failures then increases fivefold between 1930 and 1933, the time of the Great Depression, when over a third of all American banks perished. In 1933, the US Congress approves the creation of the Federal Deposit Insurance Corporation (FDIC)—one of the earliest examples of universal deposit insurance in the world. With deposit insurance in place, the number of bank failures falls dramatically over the next ten years despite the aftermath of the Great Depression. Then, over the 40-year period from 1943 to 1982, the average number of banks that required FDIC assistance was a mere seven per year— with essentially no episodes of full-blown bank runs.[1] Fair to say, deposit insurance transformed the risk profile of banking beyond recognition.

Since its first appearance more than 20 centuries earlier, banking had always been a type of business venture working under the ever-present possibility of total failure. Banks' financial structure meant their survival

---

[1] Benston (1983).

relied on the trust of their debt holders. If that trust evaporated, and debtors asked for repayment, banks went out of business. It is only during the twentieth century that an institutional infrastructure is devised for rendering this financial structure safe. Thanks to public-owned Central Banks, inconvertible currency, and deposit insurance, banks have been liberated from the ever-present risk of bank runs and have proceeded to play an increasingly prominent role in the economic life of modern society.

~~~

Having seen how the problem of bank runs was solved, let us turn our attention towards the other long-standing obstacle to the development of banking: the limit to bank deposit creation imposed by the availability of bank reserves.

When Central Banks take on the role of producers of bank reserves, the business of banking accommodates itself into a two-step procedure. In the first step, commercial banks issue liabilities called bank deposits and obtain financial assets from the public in return. The financial assets in question may take different forms: today, they are debts issued by bank borrowers directly in favour of the bank which go by the name of bank loans. In the past, banks would accept debts which had been previously issued among private agents as a result of commercial transactions.[2] Regardless of the form of these assets, the operation increases the quantity of bank deposits in the economy and, by this stroke, the amount of bank reserves needed to back them up. And since all banks are engaging in bank deposit creation simultaneously, bank reserves will need to increase at the aggregate level.

That's where the second step comes in. As we have seen before, the Central Bank is in a position to issue additional Central Bank deposits in exchange for financial assets offered by banks. During the nineteenth century, the financial assets which banks would offer were the very same debts bought from the public in the first step above. Today, Central Banks would normally accept only government bonds. This represents

---

[2] As an example, a manufacturer would buy raw material from his supplier and, instead of paying on the spot, would issue a short-term debt for the amount due. The supplier could then approach a bank and sell this debt for newly issued bank deposits. Banks bought these debts at a discount—they paid less than £100 for every £100 due—and the difference remunerated them in lieu of interest payments. Albeit indirectly, the operation allows the bank to finance the manufacturer's purchase.

no problem for commercial banks, as the procedure indicated above can be used to buy bonds from the government instead of bank loans from the public. Ultimately, the system allows banks to increase their reserves by selling some of the assets acquired via bank deposit creation. Banks will want to do this whenever their ratio of bank reserves to bank deposits is considered too low.

When convertibility of Central Bank notes into gold was in place, the above process would take place under a powerful constraint—the Central Bank was not free to issue its deposits at will. Once convertibility is abandoned, however, no further limits apply. Banks would arguably be able to back up money creation of any magnitude if the additional reserves required need not be kept in proportion to precious metal holdings. This, however, assumes that additional bank reserves will indeed be forthcoming—in other words, that the Central Bank will be willing to produce them for the benefit of commercial banks whenever asked. Whether that will indeed be the case deserves further consideration.

The Central Bank could conceivably deny requests for additional bank reserves if it wanted, forcing banks to limit the quantity of bank deposits they issue. If it did so, the Central Bank would be in a position to control money creation by banks—and, by extension, the money supply. For instance, the Central Bank could announce the quantity of Central Bank deposits it would be ready to issue over a period of time, and commercial banks would adapt the magnitude of bank deposit creation in accordance. As it turns out, it has been a central tenet of twentieth-century economics that such a state of affairs accords with reality. Standard economic analysis has viewed the money supply as a variable under the control of the Central Bank—a variable that can be increased or decreased according to the goals of public policy. The notion has been ubiquitous in economics textbooks over generations, and continues to be taught in undergraduate classes to this very day.[3]

Unfortunately, reality does not agree with the above perspective. When commercial banks confront the Central Bank with their needs for additional reserves, the Central Bank is hardly in a position to deny

---

[3] In addition, textbook treatments typically reverse the order of the actions, with the Central Bank creating bank reserves first, and commercial banks using those reserves to sustain money creation afterwards. This order is erroneous, and derives from the assumption that banks need to have reserves in place for the full amount of the loan which they intend to grant. As we have seen already, that is not the case.

them. Central Banks are established with the mission of safeguarding the stability and smooth functioning of the commercial banking system. Providing additional reserves on demand is key to the delivery of this mission, as failure to do so would quickly lead into a series of problems.

For a start, the amount of bank reserves which banks hold is subject to sudden fluctuations. This happens because bank deposits can be exchanged for currency at any time, which depletes bank reserves. If a trade fair is in town, for instance, the public may want to carry an unusually large number of transactions with cash—which translates into large currency withdrawals. Banks would react by asking the Central Bank for additional reserves in order to satisfy the public. Failure to comply may lead to a loss of confidence in the banking sector and potential bank runs, something that the Central Bank is strongly expected to avoid.

Second, banks' lending portfolio is subject to changes which are beyond their immediate control, and a sudden increase in bank lending requires a rapid inflow of additional bank reserves. This happens because commercial banks typically make lines of credit available to their customers: they pre-approve maximum loan amounts to be used in the future at the discretion of their clients. Overdrafts and credit cards are two examples of this. When a customer decides to use his line of credit, the bank cannot refuse. Failure to provide additional reserves to cover for such loan extensions would create disruption in the short term, and probably lead to the disappearance of lines of credit in the long term. It is not clear how the economy would function if firms and households did not have the possibility of using credit lines in order to bridge financing gaps.

Finally, perhaps the most overpowering reason derives from the need to stabilize the interbank market for bank reserves. Before going to the Central Bank for more reserves, banks can borrow reserves from each other in this market. Led to its own devises, this market will exhibit extreme instability of interest rates. Whenever reserves become scarce at the aggregate level, for instance because banks have been expanding their loans and creating bank deposits, the interest rate in this market will be high. Whenever reserves are abundant, for instance because the public has not been withdrawing currency as usual, the interest rate in this market will fall towards zero. The interest rate charged for bank reserves in this market has a direct influence on the interest rates offered to members of the public on their loans, as any loan may be financed in a first instance by borrowing from this market. A highly volatile interest rate on bank reserves is therefore undesirable, as it would make bank lending rates unstable and unpredictable.

The Central Bank avoids all of the above pitfalls by standing ready to supply reserves on demand against financial assets of a given quality and at a pre-determined price, expressed in terms of an interest rate. In technical jargon, the Central Bank operates a "standing facility". With this in place, the interest rate on the interbank market for bank reserves cannot be higher than the rate offered by the Central Bank. Banks would never pay each other more than 5% on borrowed reserves if they can get reserves in whatever quantity is needed from the Central Bank at that price. Typically, the interest rate on the interbank market will then fluctuate somewhere below 5%, rising temporary to the 5% limit when sudden changes in economic conditions lead to reserve scarcity. Since such scarcity is met with reserve injections from the Central Bank, the rate will soon fall back to a lower level. Over time, such periodic recourse to the Central Bank's standing facility will allow commercial banks to expand their lending portfolio at will.

Operating a standing facility was the standard practice of Central Banks throughout the nineteenth century and into the early twentieth century. A standing facility was a natural extension of the way in which commercial banks operate. Commercial banks stand ready to issue bank deposits against acceptable financial assets issued by the public, at a pre-determined interest rate. Similarly, the Central Bank stands ready to issue Central Bank deposits against acceptable financial assets at a pre-determined interest rate, only its clients are banks rather than the general public. The Central Bank may discount existing assets, or accept newly issued assets from commercial banks.

During the twentieth century, Central Banks increasingly complement the existence of a standing facility with the practice of participating in financial markets to buy and sell assets from banks. Insiders refer to such purchases and sales as "Open Market Operations". Instead of standing ready to buy assets from banks, the Central Bank would go and demand such assets directly. As the century advances, Open Market Operations become increasingly popular among Central Banks the world over—eventually becoming the tool of choice for carrying out the designs of monetary policy.

Quite unfortunately, the popularity of Open Market Operations over the last few decades has brought support to the idea that Central

Banks are in control of the quantity of bank reserves in the system—and therefore of money creation. An Open Market Operation gives the impression of a Central Bank acting independently, not leaving the quantity of assets it purchases to be determined by commercial banks. I must therefore emphasize that such is not the case. Open Market Operations still take place within the economic environment described above, which pretty much forces the Central Bank to provide the reserves the banking system needs. What Open Market Operations achieve is something rather modest. They simply preempt banks from systematically using the standing facility—thus ensuring that most transactions of bank reserves take place within the interbank market for reserves. By buying additional assets, the Central Bank makes sure this interbank market has enough reserves to satisfy all its participants. Far from acting independently, the Central Bank anticipates the needs of commercial banks and satisfies them, avoiding bottlenecks and last-minute rushes arising from the operation of the standing facility.

Whether making use of Open Market Operations or not, then, Central Bank policy has never been to direct the quantity of bank reserves in the system in an attempt to dictate money creation. With a few notable exceptions, it has always been clear to Central Banks that attempting to do so would be a fool's errand. Instead, Central Banks have always offered reserves to the banking system pretty much on demand, and searched to exercise an influence on banks, and the economy at large, by setting a higher or lower level of the interest rate on those reserves—what is referred to as "interest rate policy". With Open Market Operations, a Central Bank can announce a target for the interest rate on the interbank market for reserves, and then buy or sell securities in order to achieve the said target. This affords a higher degree of control and clarity than operating solely through a standing facility, where only an upper limit for said interest rate is set. Of course, a system based on Open Market Operations will still feature a standing facility, to resolve unanticipated reserve needs arising after the Central Bank has done its purchasing.

Using its interest rate policy, the Central Bank will typically influence the lending rates offered by commercial banks to the general public—albeit imperfectly, commercial banks pass on the cost of acquiring reserves to their clients. The Central Bank will hope to restrain lending by setting higher rates when lending is perceived as excessive, and stimulate lending by setting lower rates when lending is perceived as insufficient. Thus interest rate policy is far from trivial but, at the same time, its importance should not be overstated. The magnitude of money creation is still in the hands of commercial banks, and will depend on the willingness of the public to take more debt and the willingness of banks to grant it. The public may decide to continue borrowing in large quantities even as interest rates increase, or not to borrow at all even as interest rates fall. The Central Bank may set up the price of bank reserves, but it is the private sector who decides on their quantity.

To conclude, present-day monetary systems have evolved mechanisms to supply additional reserves to commercial banks as these expand their lending portfolio and create money. The Central Bank can make the acquisition of those reserves more or less expensive, but it cannot stop it or dictate it. With additional bank reserves always available, commercial banks have become the engine of money creation in all modern economies.

CHAPTER 8

The Role of Banks in a Modern Economy

Keywords Banks · Money creation · Financial intermediaries

Having reached the present day in our historical overview, let us take stock and advance a concise description of the monetary system in place in all modern economies, and of the very special role of banks within it.

Most economic exchange today requires the use of money, and most of this money is nothing other than bank debts which go by the name of bank deposits. Although banks can issue bank deposits upon reception of currency, the operation is of marginal importance in any modern economy and does not lead to an expansion of the money supply. Economies expand their money supply when banks issue bank deposits in exchange for private debts issued by households and firms; private debts which go by the names of bank loans, mortgages, or corporate bonds. This accounting operation is what we call bank lending.

The bank deposits thus created are transferred to other members of the public as payment for goods and services. Once these transfers are made, the bank remains creditor to the bank borrowers but now becomes debtor to the general public. A common mistake is to believe this financial structure is the result of banks borrowing money from the public and transferring it to borrowers—which amounts to getting the process

© The Author(s), under exclusive license to Springer Nature Switzerland AG 2022
L. Angeles, *Money Matters*,
https://doi.org/10.1007/978-3-030-95516-8_8

exactly the wrong way around. Banks finance borrowers by issuing money, but this money is also bank debt. When borrowers transfer this debt to members of the public, banks become debtors to them.

The capacity to create money brings to mind the possibility of untold riches. This, however, confuses money with currency—you would indeed become impossibly rich if you were able to turn paper into banknotes. The money that banks create, however, is nothing other than bank debts—and issuing debts tends to make you poorer rather than richer. This is the case for bank deposits, which are due a certain interest payment and, in addition, force the bank to provide costly payment services for them. Having said that, banks are far from losing out in the bargain. Banks receive assets in exchange for the money they create, and these assets pay a handsome interest rate. The resulting interest income covers the cost of servicing bank deposits plus all costs involved in originating the loans: screening loan applicants, handling all transactions, satisfying legal requirements, etc. Judging by the salaries in the banking industry, a considerable surplus is still in place after all this.

Most people—including highly educated individuals, business leaders, politicians, stock market analysts, and even professional economists— make two fundamental mistakes when thinking about money and banking.

The first mistake is to think that money is some form of public good—like street lighting, paved roads, or schooling. Public goods are provided by a government, typically free of charge, and are financed by taxation. Their supply is guided by the benefits to society at large, but can be distorted by the forces intervening in the political process. Their production does not result in private profits.

Money is nothing like that. Money creation results from the free interaction between private borrowers and commercial banks. Banks cannot create money at will: they are only able to do so if there is a firm or a household willing to borrow it. In this operation, both bank and bank borrower are moved by the possibility of private gains: banks earn interest income, while borrowers can generate profits or achieve a more desirable consumption schedule. Money creation and the financing of borrowers can be hugely beneficial to society, but the benefits to society are not in the minds of the actors involved. Paraphrasing the great Adam Smith, banks and borrowers, by pursuing their own interests, frequently promote the interest of society more effectually than when they really intend to promote it.

The second mistake has been already mentioned but is worth developing in more detail: the idea that banks are financial intermediaries, transferring money from people who want to save to firms and households who want to borrow. The view is a remnant of the practice of ancient banking, when currency in the form of precious metal coins was the only form of money available and had to be transferred from savers to borrowers. Banks started to move away from this practice more than six centuries ago, and had completely abandoned it by the turn of the twentieth century. It is a remarkable anomaly that most well-educated people continue to hang on to it.

To be sure, financial intermediation exists and is an important part of the financial architecture in any modern economy—pension funds and insurance companies are two of the most important examples of financial intermediaries. Financial intermediaries collect money from the public by issuing liabilities which are non-monetary, and use the money received to buy assets on financial markets—mostly stocks and bonds. When they do so, they transfer money to the seller of these instruments—and ultimately to the firms that issued them. By doing this, financial intermediaries offer an alternative source of financing for firms, one that is often cheaper and less constraining than bank lending. While most small- and medium-sized firms rely entirely on bank finance, large firms often prefer to raise funds using financial intermediation instead.

A crucial limitation of financial intermediaries, however, is that they can only allocate the funds which the public agrees to lend to them, whereas banks create the funds they loan. As a consequence, bank finance is typically far more important as a source of funds than financial intermediation—and, indeed, the only source of external funds for households, who do not issue bonds or stocks.

One of the reasons why the nature of modern banks is so commonly misunderstood, is that the business of an individual bank, when considered in isolation, does look like financial intermediation. A bank manager knows that, upon approval of a loan, the bank will issue a deposit in favour of the borrower. This deposit, however, only stays for a very short time in the bank's books—it will be transferred to other banks as soon as the borrower uses it. In many cases, such as mortgages or credit card loans, these two operations are in fact simultaneous. As soon as it makes the loan, then, the bank must worry about obtaining inflows of funds which will counteract this outflow—ideally, inflows of bank deposits. From the perspective of the individual bank, new deposits need to be found in order to finance the loans made. If you speak to bank managers, they are likely to tell you that banks can only transfer the funds that they receive.

What bank managers fail to see is the aggregate picture. The incoming deposits which each bank hopes to attract were created by the other banks in the system when granting loans. Banks compete for the funds available, but the funds themselves are of their own creation. If we look at the banking system as a whole, so that movements of deposits between banks cancel out, loans are being financed by the deposits which the banking system has itself created. We cannot understand money creation by looking at a single bank in isolation. The aggregate picture is necessary to grasp the nature of the system.

While we all agree that banks are important institutions, the full magnitude of their role often goes unappreciated. Since most people regard banks as financial intermediaries, they only assign them importance in allocating the funds entrusted to them by the public—plus being in charge of the payments system. But banks are far more important than this. Their actions impact not only the allocation of funds, but the total quantity of funds available to be allocated. They make possible the expansion of the money supply, which has consequences that go well beyond the financing of households and firms, as we shall see in the rest of this book.

Banks are the central element of a complex system which, like every other complex system we know of, is the outcome of endogenous evolution—not exogenous design. It looks the way it does because, over a period of centuries and millennia, private and public actors have interacted with each other in the monetary and economic arena, faced different challenges, and progressively found solutions to these challenges. The outcome of this lengthy process is a monetary system that works pretty well, as it has cumulated successful innovations and discarded unsuccessful ones over a very long period. The system might not be perfect, but most households and firms are able to obtain financing when they need it, billions of payments take place every day without a glitch, and money is provided to the economy in adequate quantities. Keep these benefits in mind as we move on to consider how our monetary and banking system can also sometimes malfunction, leading us into considerable trouble.

PART II

An Analysis of Financial Crises

CHAPTER 9

The Role of Money and the Logic of Recessions

Keywords Credit to the private sector · Recession · External shocks · Money-based economies · Savings · Circular flow of money

There is no denying the importance of the financial system for the health and progress of any modern economy. This is true for the many markets and financial intermediaries that constitute the system—the bond and stock markets, the markets for financial derivatives, the insurance companies, the wealth management companies—but, most of all, this is true for the banking system.

Previous chapters have indicated why banks are so important. They finance the vast majority of borrowers—making it possible for many firms to invest and for most households to smooth their consumption over their lifetimes. Banks handle all payments in an economy and, as the economy grows, they supply the additional money it needs. A quick look at macroeconomic aggregates reveals that, as a rule, economic development is accompanied by the expansion of the business of banking.

Figure 9.1 offers good evidence of this last assertion. The figure plots a standard measure of economic development (GDP per capita, calculated on a purchasing power parity basis) against a measure of the overall development of the financial sector for the world's 40 largest economies.

L. Angeles, *Money Matters*, https://doi.org/10.1007/978-3-030-95516-8_9

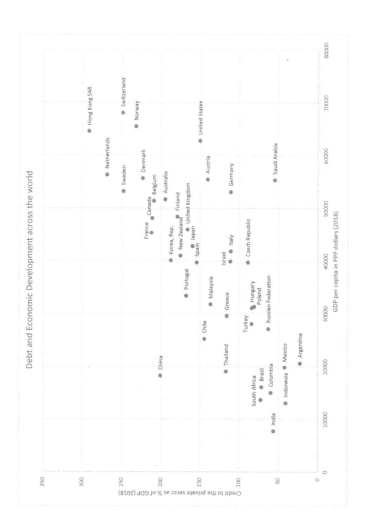

Fig. 9.1 Debt and economic development across the world (*Sources* Bank for International Settlements [credit to GDP ratio], World Bank [GDP per capita])

Financial sector development is measured by credit to the private sector as a percent of GDP—in other words, the sum of all debts owed by firms and households, from all available sources, normalized by the size of the economy. For the average country, 94% of all this debt is owed to banks—credit to the private sector is essentially a measure of bank lending.[1]

Figure 9.1 shows a clear positive gradient between level of development and bank lending: richer countries are also countries where households and firms have larger debts in proportion to their income. The relationship is linear and pretty tight for this type of data. We may note that China has too much debt for its level of income while Saudi Arabia has too little, but most countries find themselves close to an imaginary line running from India and Indonesia (low-income and low-debt levels) to Switzerland, Hong Kong, or Norway (high-income and high-debt levels). As countries develop, then, their banking sector becomes more and more important—a good indication that banks assist society in the process of economic development, and that a larger and more complex financial sector is part and parcel of how economies grow.

Banks, however, are hardly admired institutions. The polling firm Gallup tracks the trust of American citizens in the most important institutions of their country. During the years 2009–2012, less than one-quarter of Americans reported trust in banks—a poor performance, placing banks as less trustworthy institutions than the Police or the Presidency, and on a par with TV news. The reason for this suspicion is not hard to figure out since banks had enjoyed much higher levels of trust just a few years earlier, up until 2008. That year saw the arrival of what became known as the global financial crisis, and a broad agreement in society that banks were largely to blame for it.

Is this assessment correct—did banks "cause" the global financial crisis? Do the benefits of banking come attached with a nasty surprise, in the form of recurrent financial mayhem? The answer will require some elaboration. We need to understand the mechanics of financial crises in order to assess the role of banks in them—let us not blame banks for causing something whose causes we don't understand. Before proceeding, however, we will need to step back and consider the role of money within the modern economy, and how it relates to the ebbs and flows of economic

---

[1] Dell'Arriccia et al. (2016, p. 303).

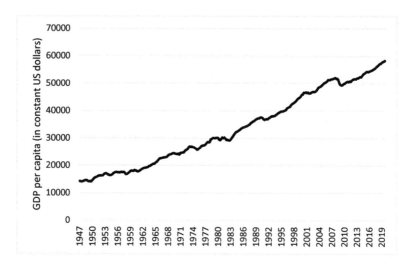

Fig. 9.2 GDP per capita of the United States, 1947–2019 (*Source* Federal Reserve Economic Data)

activity. Financial crises are a monetary phenomenon with vast implications on the economy's real side—on production, employment, and trade. I need to make clear how money relates to the real side of the economy under normal circumstances, before we can consider how this relationship behaves under the worst possible circumstances.

Figure 9.2 presents the evolution of GDP per capita in the United States over the period 1947–2019. The figure gives us a good illustration of the process of economic growth as it takes place in the absence of major shocks such as civil wars, foreign invasions, health pandemics, and the like. A comparable picture would characterize all countries living under adequate conditions of peace and social order.

Two characteristics of the process are immediately evident from this figure. First, there is an unmistakable tendency for economies to grow over the medium to long term. The normal state of affairs is for economies to get richer and richer over time, and for average incomes to increase accordingly. The force behind this tendency is technological progress: each year we build up on last year's pool of productive knowledge, and become better and better at producing everything from smartphones to legal services.

The second characteristic of the process of economic growth is that it is not completely smooth: the rate of economic expansion varies, and can be negative in some particular years. Periods of positive growth are regularly interrupted by periods of contraction when economic activity falls, unemployment increases, and people become less well-off. We refer to these recurrent periods of economic malaise as recessions.

There would be no mystery regarding recessions if they were caused by negative external shocks such as natural disasters. In a poor developing country, for instance, a year with insufficient rains may ruin much of the crops and result in a major recession. Or an earthquake may destroy some key areas of a country's infrastructure—roads, airports, harbours— and bring much economic production to a halt. We refer to such shocks as "external" because they originate outside the economy—they do not result from the actions of households, firms or the government. These external shocks are certainly a tragedy, but the resulting recession is clearly no mystery.

External shocks can be the cause of recessions in poor developing countries but, crucially, they are never behind major recessions in the world's advanced economies. Large and rich economies are too diverse and resilient to be severely affected by weather, and agricultural production is a very small part of their total output in any case. And while earthquakes and volcanoes can cause some damage, the infrastructure of rich countries can easily find solutions to the loss of one particular road or harbour. In the world's advanced economies recessions typically take place in the absence of any damage to productive capacity: no loss of infrastructure, no reduction in available capital or machinery, no changes in the labour force—and certainly, no technological regression. Plainly, the economy would still be capable of producing the same level of output as in the recent past but, for some reason, it simply fails to do so. Now that is a mystery.

For reasons we are yet to uncover, economies seem to engender recessions from within themselves—in the parlance of economists, the causes are "endogenous" (from within the system) rather than external. And, as I shall argue below, the causes arise from the very nature of all money-based economies. If the economy uses money to facilitate exchange, the risk of endogenous recessions is present.

A money-based economy is an economy where people sell their labour against money, and use the money received to buy goods and services in a market. People typically sell their labour to firms, who use the labour to produce goods and services—the very same goods and services which are then sold to people. Money thus circulates from firms to households in the form of wage payments, and from households back to firms in the form of payments for goods and services. Money changes hands in markets (the labour market, the markets for goods and services), and markets are at the centre of all economic activity.

The opposite of a money-based economy would be an economy with no markets. Imagine an economy where every household uses its labour to produce goods and services for its own consumption—or for the consumption of a local lord or religious authority who taxes their production in kind. Such an economy would have no need for money or markets since all production is either consumed directly or transferred for others to consume. No economy in history has ever functioned entirely along these lines, but large parts of Europe during the height of feudalism would have approached it.

Europe leaves this stage during the late Middle Ages, as an ever larger share of production is bought and sold in markets. Markets, however, were hampered by an insufficient supply of universally accepted means of payment—in other words, precious metal coins were rather rare. As we have seen, societies adapted to these circumstances by arranging exchange via the establishment and subsequent cancellation of bilateral debts. The method makes exchange possible between parties who are familiar with each other, but what of exchange between parties who have never met (or, having met, do not trust each other)? Impersonal market exchange, exchange between pairs of strangers, cannot be based on bilateral debts. The development of fully fledged market economies, then, is conditional on an adequate supply of money.

The great advantage of market economies where all exchange is money-based is that you can consume the produce of anyone's labour and pay for it by supplying the produce of your own labour *to anybody else*. This is far more powerful than allowing a butcher and a brewer to exchange meat and beer with each other by means of bilateral debts—an easy task, since most butchers will want some beer and most brewers will want some meat. A money-based market economy allows a philosophy professor to obtain his meat and beer even if no butcher or brewer in town is interested in philosophy lessons. As long as someone somewhere is interested in philosophy, and is ready to pay for lessons with ready money, our professor will be able to sell the product of his labour to society and use the proceeds to buy his lunch. The market pulls out such improbable exchanges as philosophy lessons for meat and beer several billion times, every single day, without anyone ever having to plan for them.

With this great advantage, however, comes a particular kind of weakness. A money-based market economy operates admirably most of the time but, on occasion, it is capable of malfunction. Most recessions are the results of such inbuilt imperfection—the system's Achilles' heel, as it were.

The operation of any money-based economy depends on people's willingness to spend the money they earn. Money, after all, can very well *not* be spent as well as it can be spent. Economists say that one of the functions of money is to serve as a store of value—to make use of this function, people must take the decision of not spending their money. The sum of all spending in an economy is referred to as aggregate expenditure, and corresponds to the flow of money from households back to firms. Money earned and not spent we call savings. Savings interrupt the flow of money from households back to firms, and reduce aggregate expenditure. When households spend less, firms will sell less. And when firms sell less, they take the decision to produce less as well—in other words, they lay off people, buy less materials, reduce investment plans, and so on. When that happens, a recession ensues.

Such a simple mechanism ought to be well understood by most people, but that is not the case. People have a surprisingly hard time accepting that savings can lead to deficiencies in aggregate expenditure because most savings are held in the form of bank deposits, and banks are supposed to transfer these savings to other agents in the economy. This, once again, is an instance where an inability to appreciate the correct nature of money and banks plays havoc with our understanding.

Most money in circulation is in the form of bank deposits—created, as we have seen, when banks make loans. It follows that most decisions not to spend money are decisions not to use bank deposits to buy goods and services. Most money saved, then, will take the form of bank deposits which we decide to leave in our name. A misunderstanding arises, however, if we believe these bank deposits are the result of currency having been saved and deposited at a bank, and that banks subsequently loan this currency to borrowers. If that were the case, the currency we save would be spent by bank borrowers, leaving overall expenditures unchanged. Even economists are liable to this form of fallacy, in particular when they think about banking using models without money. In such models, savings are in the form of real resources—and banks are in the business of collecting these savings and transferring them to borrowers. Banks in models without money, then, are not engaged in what we have referred to as *modern banking*—they practice a form of *ancient banking* instead.

Having said this, it is of course possible for us to lend some of our savings to other people—either directly or using a financial intermediary. The important thing to realize is that there is nothing automatic about this: we may decide to save and keep our money in the form of bank deposits, or we may decide to save and use these bank deposits to, for instance, invest in the stockmarket—in which case we transfer our savings to somebody else. The decision to save some of our income and the decision to use some of those savings to invest are separate decisions—it is not the case that all savings are transferred. Money that has been saved and transferred will be spent by somebody else in the economy and will not result in a reduction of aggregate expenditure. But equally, money that has been saved and is not transferred will not be spent, and will cause aggregate expenditure to fall.

The bottom line, then, is that the circular flow of money from firms to households and from households back to firms *can* be interrupted. Such interruptions will leave goods and services unsold and signal firms to lay off employees and reduce production. A coordinated decision of all households not to spend their money, and spend their days basking in the sun instead, would send the economy into the mother of all recessions.

Are recessions then caused by people suddenly refusing to spend their money? In short, no—people do not behave this way. Cultural critics may relish in their attacks against consumerism, but the public rarely listens. Most people spend most of their income in consumption, most of the time.

On the other hand, people often react to poor economic prospects by becoming more cautious with their spending. If an economy experiences a slowdown for some reason, so that people expect difficult times ahead, postponing major expenditures is a common reaction. People won't buy a new car, or book an expensive holiday, if they fear for their jobs over the coming months. They will put some extra money aside, in case regular income falters. By doing so, they contribute to any initial decline in expenditures already in place, making a budding recession all the worse. Thus, changes in the public's willingness to spend are very likely a consequence of recessions, and they help to explain why recessions reach the magnitude and severity they do. But changes in the public's willingness to spend are an unlikely *prime mover* behind most recessions. People like spending money, and their appetite for consumption follows well-established norms and habits. We should not look into recurrent cycles of frugality as an explanation for recurrent recessions.

My aim over the next few chapters is not to offer a universal explanation for why recessions take place. Most likely, the causes are manifold and change according to the country and period we consider. What I will offer, on the other hand, is what may be considered a universal explanation for why financial crises take place, and why they lead to large recessions. The mechanism just expounded, linking the expenditure of money to economic activity, will play a central role in this explanation.

CHAPTER 10

Describing Financial Crises

Keywords Financial crises · Global financial crisis · Asian financial crisis · Nordic banking crisis · Deleveraging · House prices · Financial liberalization

Recessions have been studied extensively within the academic literature. In a paper published in 2013, Oscar Jorda, Moritz Schularick, and Alan M. Taylor identify every single recession episode taking place in the 14 most important high-income economies (the United States, Japan, Canada, Australia, and ten Western European nations) since the year 1870.[1] They classify recessions into two varieties: common recessions and financial crises recessions. A financial crisis is defined as an episode where a large number of the country's banks face serious trouble, with sharp increases in non-performing loans and severe losses of bank capital. Many of these episodes are characterized by bank runs, the introduction of a freeze on all currency withdrawals from banks, and widespread financial support and intervention by the Central Bank or other public authority. Their sample contains 173 common recessions and 50 financial crises recessions.

---

[1] Jorda et al. (2013).

L. Angeles, *Money Matters*,
https://doi.org/10.1007/978-3-030-95516-8_10

Table 10.1 Path of GDP per capita, normal recessions vs. financial crisis recessions

	Year 1	Year 2	Year 3	Year 4	Year 5
Normal recession	−2.0	0.0	+2.0	+3.3	+4.5
Financial crisis recession	−2.7	−3.1	−2.5	−0.9	+1.0

Note The figures show the average change in GDP per capita in percentage terms between the onset of the recession ("Year 0") and each of the five subsequent years. Averages are taken across 173 normal recession episodes and 50 financial crisis episodes. *Source* Jorda et al. (2013, p. 13)

Using this study, Table 10.1 provides a straight comparison between the two varieties of recessions. The table reports the change in GDP per capita in percentage terms between the onset of the recession ("Year 0") and each of the subsequent five years ("Year 1" to "Year 5"). The figures represent the average outcome across all recessions and crises studied. As we see, a common recession tends to last only one year. GDP per capita is on average 2% lower one year after it begins, but is back to its pre-crisis level by the second year and continues to grow from there onwards. A financial crisis, on the other hand, is a far more protracted affair. In the average case, GDP per capita remains below its pre-crisis level for a full four years. If we compare the path of GDP per capita under the two scenarios, a financial crisis leads to a loss of 16% of GDP per capita over five years in excess of the loss from a normal recession.[2] Financial crises are not just more damaging than common recessions—they are several times more damaging.

The largest financial crises last considerably longer than four years and are considerably more damaging. Japan's financial crisis in the year 1990 led to a period of weak economic growth that is commonly referred to as Japan's "lost decade"—a period which, despite its name, lasts considerably longer than ten years. Similarly, following the global financial crisis of 2008, several European countries did not regain their pre-crisis level of economic activity until the middle of the next decade. During the year following the onset of this crisis, industrial production fell by a whopping 30% in Japan, and by close to 20% in both Europe and the United

---

[2] Calculated by taking the difference between the loss under a financial crisis recession and the loss under a normal recession for each of the first five years, and adding up.

States. Unemployment soared from 2.6 to 8% of the labour force in the United Kingdom, from around 5% to almost 10% in the United States, and from around 7.5 to 12% or more in the Euro Zone. When it comes to economic dislocation and distress, a major financial crisis is hard to beat.

Financial crises have been a topic of academic study for several decades, and much more so since 2008. The empirical side of this research programme has borne good fruit: today, we understand quite a lot about the usual outline of financial crises—their external features, so to speak. Financial crises tend to follow a typical script. In this script, banks play arguably the leading role—or share this distinction with bank borrowers.

Financial crises take place following large and rapid increases in the magnitude of bank lending. Economists have uncovered this relationship by running statistical analyses where a battery of macroeconomic indicators is used to try to predict the onset of a financial crisis. Overwhelmingly, the variable with most predictive power tends to be the growth rate of a measure we have encountered already: credit to the private sector, as a percent of GDP. As was mentioned, credit to the private sector is composed almost entirely of debts owed to the banking sector. Changes in private credit over GDP tell us how fast banks are expanding their lending portfolio in relation to the overall economy. If the economy is growing at a rate of 5% per year, banks expanding their lending portfolio by 5% as well would leave this measure unchanged—and would be no cause for concern. If banks instead expand their lending by say 15%, and do so repeatedly over several years, a financial crisis becomes ever more likely.[3]

But the relationship between credit expansion and financial crises goes beyond this anticipation effect. The empirical literature has not only found that credit expansion is followed by crisis, but that larger expansions in credit are followed by deeper, more damaging crises. Figure 10.1 presents graphical evidence of this pertaining to the global financial crisis of 2008. The figure displays, on its horizontal axis, the increase in the ratio of credit to GDP during the build-up phase of the crisis— the period 2002–2007. On the vertical axis we read a measure of the severity of the crisis: the increase in the unemployment rate between 2007

---

[3] For research work featuring this finding see Schularick and Taylor (2012), Jorda et al. (2013), Mian and Sufi (2010), Mian et al. (2017), IMF (2012, 2017). Some of these works emphasize the importance of household debt (as opposed to firm debt).

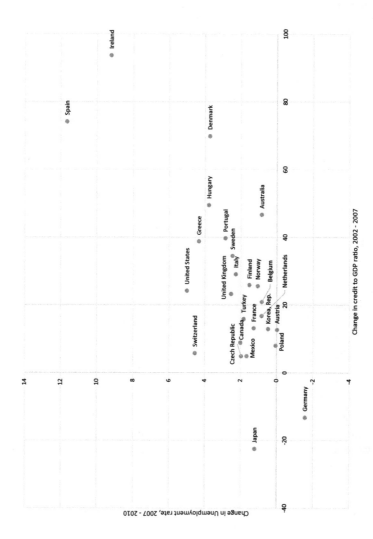

Fig. 10.1 Growth in debt and severity of subsequent crisis, Global Financial Crisis episode (*Source* Dataset from Mian et al. 2017)

and 2010. The resulting scatter plot shows a distinct positive relationship between these two magnitudes. Countries where bank credit expanded the most, such as Spain and Ireland, were also the countries that saw the steepest increases in unemployment. Countries where bank credit expanded the least or even contracted, such as Germany, were also the countries where unemployment did not rise by much or, in the case of Germany, even decreased. Other countries find themselves somewhere in between these two extremes.

Findings such as those displayed in Table 10.1 and Fig. 10.1 are the result of empirical analyses carried out using a large number of countries, often observed over a long period of time. Such an empirical methodology is necessary if we want to identify the typical characteristics of financial crises. To bring these general results to life, however, it will be useful to pass in review some of the most prominent examples of financial crises around the world over the last forty years. This will also give us a chance to introduce a number of additional regularities we observe, and which are not so easily picked up by statistical analysis. Our attention will be focused on developed economies. There have been only three outbreaks of financial crises within these countries over the last forty years, and we are able to cover all three in what follows. Financial crises in developing countries have been too numerous to attempt a comprehensive coverage, but I do present the case of the Asian Financial Crisis of 1997—arguably the most substantial episode to take place in the developing world, and the one affecting the largest number of countries.

To begin, however, let us take a look at the United States. The United States provides a good benchmark from where to judge other countries given its large and diverse economy and highly developed financial system. Figure 10.2 presents the evolution of credit to the private sector as a percent of GDP from 1952 to the present. The figure gives a good summary view of how the financial side of an economy may be expected to evolve: credit to GDP typically grows steadily over time—in the case of the United States, from a value of around 60% during the 1950s to around 150% today. Most of the time, the ratio appears to evolve along a linear trend. The dotted line represents the linear function which best fits the data, and the fit is a remarkably good one. Up until the year 2000, most realized values of the credit to GDP ratio fell close to the values which this line predicts. Over most of the post-war period, then, the American financial system was growing ever larger with respect to the size of the economy but the growth appeared predictable and steady.

Fig. 10.2 Credit to the private sector in the United States, 1952–2019 (*Source* Bank for International Settlements)

Things change, however, around the turn of the twenty-first century. Beginning in the late 1990s, the growth of private credit far outpaces its historical trend. This rapid growth is sustained for about a decade so that, by the year 2007, the ratio of credit to GDP is some 20% points higher than what would be predicted by its linear trend. The peak of this ratio coincides with the onset of the global financial crisis. Over the next few years, a highly unusual phenomenon takes place: credit to GDP decreases. Indeed, starting from 2008, the economy enters into a phase of *aggregate deleveraging*: banks grant far fewer new loans than in previous years while existing loans become due for repayment. The level of private debt decreases, resulting in a rapid fall in the ratio of credit to GDP. A look at Fig. 10.2 tells us that the magnitude of aggregate deleveraging taking place post-2008 was unprecedented at least since the 1950s. Private deleveraging continues until the year 2015—a period which largely coincides with low economic activity and high levels of unemployment.

Figure 10.2 also reveals that the dynamic encountered during the first decade of the twenty-first century was anticipated by a movement of similar shape but lesser magnitude during the 1980s. This corresponds to the crisis of America's Savings and Loans Associations—a type of financial institution specializing in the provision of mortgages and other types of loans to households. The episode is usually characterized by experts as a "borderline" financial crisis, as the size of Savings & Loans Associations was substantial but not as important as that of the commercial banking system. The turn of America's banking system would come, only two decades later.

Figure 10.3 keeps the United States in the picture and adds two economies which were also greatly affected by the global financial crisis of 2008: the United Kingdom and Spain. We notice the evolution of credit to GDP in these two countries is less predictable than in the United States—it does not tend to follow a linear path. Nevertheless, and just as in the United States, the decade preceding the global financial crisis stands out as a period of unprecedented growth in this measure. In Britain, credit to the private sector passes from around 120% of GDP to 190% between 1998 and 2008. In Spain the trajectory is even more dramatic, passing from 80% of GDP to well over 200% over the same period. The pattern we observe in these three countries was repeated in a number of other economies across the world: the global financial crisis took place on the eve of very rapid expansions in the lending activity of banks in a number

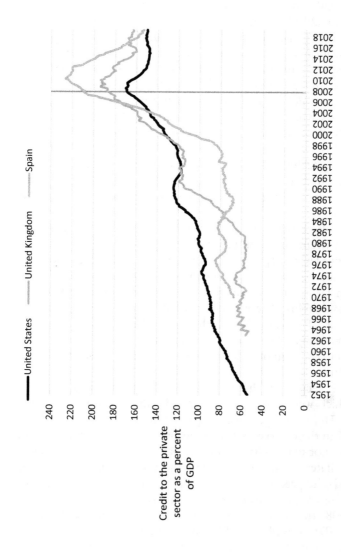

Fig. 10.3 The Global Financial Crisis of 2008: the United States, the United Kingdom, and Spain (*Source* Bank for International Settlements)

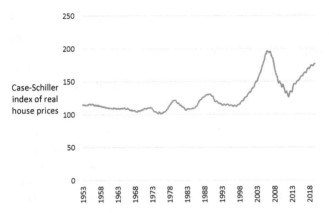

Fig. 10.4 Real house prices in the United States, 1953–2019 (*Source* econ. yale.edu/~shiller/)

of advanced economies. And, as the cases of the United States, the United Kingdom, and Spain illustrate, this was succeeded by several years of debt deleveraging across the world.

That, however, is not the only similarity. As is well known, together with the expansion of bank lending these economies experienced a sustained boom in house prices—let us review some of the evidence regarding this phenomenon as well. For the United States, the Case-Schiller house price index aggregates data on different types of properties across the whole country and divides house prices by an index of consumer prices. The result is what economists refer to as a real price index: a measure that increases not when house prices increase (which happens nearly all the time), but when houses prices increase with respect to the price of all other goods and services in the economy. The opposite applies when the measure decreases.

Figure 10.4 presents the evolution of this index from 1953 to the present. We notice that, up until the late 1990s, house prices did no more than increase in line with other prices in the economy. There were periods of relatively rapid house price growth (increasing index), but these were not long-lived and were regularly succeeded by periods of relatively slow house price growth (decreasing index). The index takes a value of around 115 in 1953, and this same value prevails by the year 1998. Over the next ten years, however, something fundamentally different happens. The index shoots up to values never seen before, reaching a peak of 195 by mid-2006. This, let's not forget, is a national average. Particular states and cities saw house price increases far in excess of these figures.

The boom was followed by a bust which brought the house price index down to 125 by the year 2012—most of the gain in real prices over the previous decade was lost. Since then house prices have regained momentum though at a less frenetic pace—it is anyone's guess whether another cycle of boom and bust is in store for the near future.

What is clear, however, is that a similar phenomenon of astonishing price increases characterized the real estate market of other economies. The average price paid for a house during the first quarter of 1998 in the United Kingdom was £78,000. During 2008 this figure reached £233,000.[4] These are nominal prices, but the increase is several times larger than price increases in other areas of the economy. The same is true for Spain, where an index of nominal house prices passes from 0.93 in 1997 to 2.17 in 2007.[5] British house prices stagnate during the decade following the year 2008, whereas Spanish house prices—as in the American case—fall by about 40% before starting a recovery.

Let's keep the above in mind as we move to observe other crises. Figure 10.5 displays credit to GDP ratios for an episode which developed from the mid-1980s into the early 1990s—the Nordic Financial Crisis (often referred to as the Nordic Banking Crisis), affecting Finland, Norway, and Sweden. Up until the early 80s, all three economies were characterized by stable ratios of credit to GDP, which had barely changed in Sweden since the 1960s and had been increasing moderately in Finland and Norway since the mid-1970s. All this changed during the 1980s, when a series of reforms deregulated the activities of banks and other financial institutions in a number of dimensions. The policy change is known in the literature as financial liberalization, and was a common move in countries throughout the world over the last two decades of the twentieth century. This was a time when faith in the powers of unregulated markets run high, and standard advice in international fora leaned strongly in favour of deregulation.

Following financial liberalization, the evolution of bank lending takes a marked turn. In all three countries, credit to GDP increases by between

---

[4] Source: Office for National Statistics (UK).

[5] Source: Jorda, Schularick and Taylor Macrohistory Dataset (Release 4).

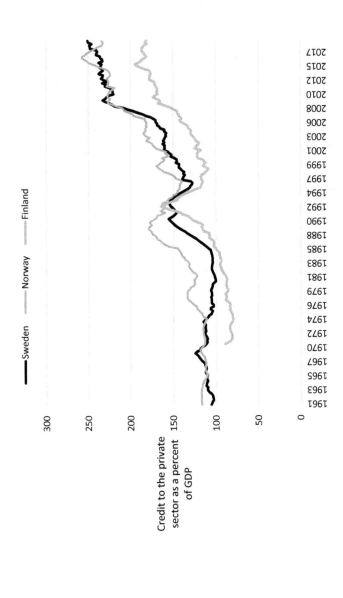

Fig. 10.5 The Nordic Financial Crisis (*Source* Bank for International Settlements)

50 and 60 percentage points over a mere five years—starting in 1985 in Sweden and Finland and somewhat earlier in Norway. This trend is reversed in 1989 for Norway, 1991 for Sweden, and 1992 for Finland, with credit to GDP ratios falling markedly following each of these years. Deleveraging led to widespread problems in the banking systems of these countries, forcing governments to intervene heavily to support them. The episode is also characterized by major recessions, compromising income and employment levels over the first half of the 1990s in all three nations.

As was the case during the build-up to the global financial crisis, the Nordic episode was preceded by large increases in house prices—in this particular case, these were truly off the charts. According to the IMF, indices of real estate prices for these three countries increased by 300% over the 1980s in Norway and Finland, and by an eye-watering 800% or more in Sweden.[6] After the crisis hit, house prices came full circle to their early-1980s values.

Finally, consider Fig. 10.6 which encompasses two separate financial crisis episodes: Japan in the year 1990, and the Asian Financial Crisis of 1997. The latter episode had serious effects on at least seven East Asian economies (and lesser effects in the rest of the region), and is represented here by two of its most prominent victims: Thailand and South Korea. Despite taking place in a very different geographic region and among economies of different income levels than those considered so far, these crises follow a similar outline as those already seen.

The Japanese crisis of 1990 was preceded by financial liberalization in Japan during the early 1980s, while the Asian Financial Crisis was preceded by financial liberalization between the late 1980s and the early 1990s taking place in most East Asian nations—including Thailand, Indonesia, Korea, Malaysia, and the Philippines.[7] In the case of middle-income countries such as Thailand and Korea at the time, financial liberalization made particular emphasis on its international side: opening the domestic economy to foreign banks, and allowing domestic firms to borrow from abroad. This was a typical aspect of the process when put in place by less-developed economies, whose domestic banking systems were less ready than foreign ones to expand their lending. It is worth

---

[6] Drees and Pazarbasioglu (1998, p. 23).

[7] See Ranciere et al. (2006, p. 3346).

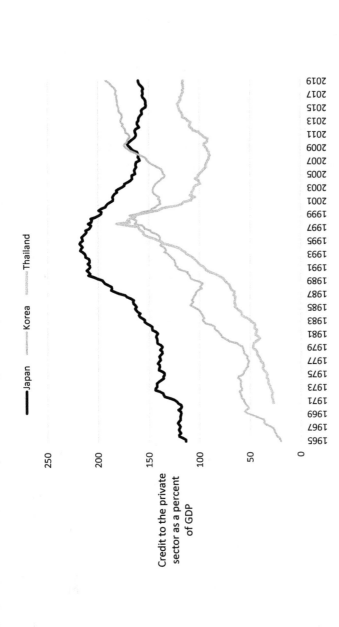

Fig. 10.6 The Japanese Crisis of 1990 and the Asian Financial Crisis of 1997 (*Source* Bank for International Settlements)

mentioning that such policies were pursued with the explicit endorsement of international institutions, notably the IMF.

The symptoms witnessed elsewhere in the wake of financial liberalizations were quick to manifest themselves in these countries as well. In Japan, credit to the private sector had been stable at 140% of GDP throughout the 1970s. By the end of the 1980s it had increased beyond 200%. Thailand had been on an upward trajectory whereby credit increased from around 30% of GDP in the early 70s to 65% of GDP in the late 80s—not unreasonable for an economy moving from low-income to middle-income status. Between 1987 and 1997, however, credit to the private sector passed from 65% to a peak of 180% of GDP—well in excess of the value that could be observed in high-income economies such as the United States or the United Kingdom at the time. Korea, finally, is perhaps a less clear-cut case since the increase in credit to GDP during the 90s, while very large, was not too dissimilar from what had happened in the country over the previous decades. It was still the case, however, that with a ratio of credit to GDP of 160% in 1998 Korea was beyond the values observed in rich Western economies.

As elsewhere, the Asian Financial Crisis brought several years of debt deleveraging to these economies—the decrease in the ratio of credit to GDP being much more marked in the Thai case than in the Korean case. Deleveraging was accompanied by a deep recession halting the rapid progress of these economies over several years. Japan is a particular case since the year 1990 marked the end of a boom period in Japan's stock and real estate markets, but private indebtedness did not begin to decrease. Instead, Japan's credit to GDP ratio stabilized and continued almost unchanged over the next seven years, with widespread banking disruption taking place only from 1997 onwards. From there on, Japan's credit to GDP went into a downward trajectory which saw it falling by 50% points over the next ten years, and has remained roughly stable ever since. The performance of the Japanese economy following its 1990 turnaround has been weak. Albeit GDP per capita rarely diminished, Japan never regained the dynamism which characterized its economy over the preceding decades, and which had seen the country elevate itself to the rank of second largest economy in the world.

Finally, the real estate market was once again behaving in an explosive fashion across all these Asian episodes. In Japan, an index of land prices for the six largest cities increases by more than 400% during the decade of the 1980s. The fall from this peak was particularly brutal: Japanese land prices lost 87% of their value between 1990 and the beginning of the twenty-first century.[8] A similar landscape could be described for the countries involved in the Asian Financial Crisis.

To summarize, a consistent pattern is in place when it comes to financial crises. Financial crises are typically preceded by large and rapid increases in bank lending. Credit to the private sector as a percent of GDP, a measure which is usually stable or slowly increasing over time, shows marked acceleration for several years in a row. Once the crisis hits, the economy enters a phase of aggregate deleveraging: firms and households reduce their debts, and credit to GDP falls. This phase is accompanied by a profound recession.

The initial expansion in bank lending sometimes coincides with the onset of financial liberalization—regulatory reforms which enhance the range of action of financial institutions in general, and the banking system in particular. In developing countries, this usually meant enhancing the range of action of foreign banks in the domestic economy. In addition, the period when the crisis is building up is normally characterized by frenetic activity and rapidly increasing prices in the real estate market. This boom in prices is spectacularly reversed once the crisis hits. Albeit I have not illustrated this in the preceding discussion, local stock markets typically follow a similar pattern as real estate markets—booming during the build-up, and taking a dip once the crisis hits. Not all financial crises will present all of the above features, but the largest among them—and every single episode taking place in developed economies over the last forty years—has closely followed this pattern.

I finish by stressing that most of the evidence just presented is uncontroversial—substantial agreement exists among researchers about the external characteristics of financial crises. The same cannot be said, however, about their underlying causes. It is widely suspected that excessive bank lending causes financial crises, but researchers have not agreed on the specific mechanism that would explain this link. Developing such a mechanism is the task we turn to next.

---

[8] Koo (2008, pp. 13 and 23).

CHAPTER 11

The Mechanics of Financial Crises—Part One

Keywords Aggregate expenditure · Spare capacity · Full capacity · Interest payments · Loan repayments

Conventional wisdom has it that financial crises are a very complex phenomenon. I beg to differ. While there may be substantial complexity in the details setting one crisis aside from another, I believe the same simple mechanism lies at the core of all of them.

This claim of simplicity does not square well with the diversity of opinions and the lack of consensus that characterizes the debate about financial crises in academia and policy circles. The reason for this, as will become apparent in what follows, is that understanding financial crises has as a prerequisite understanding money and banking. Get money and banking right, and you are only a modest step away from piercing the logic of financial crises. Get money and banking wrong, and your quest to explain financial crises will likely get lost along blind alleys.

Back in Chapter 8, I highlighted the importance of banks by noting that they don't just allocate funds to borrowers but create the funds to be allocated—in the form of newly issued bank deposits. Chapter 9 then described the logic at the centre of all money-based economies: money circulates from firms to households when production takes place, and from households back to firms when consumption takes place. Put these two elements together and you realize that money does not circulate within a closed loop. New injections of money are constantly entering the economic body through the actions of banks. When this happens, households and firms are able to spend more money than they would otherwise have been able to. The additional expenditure which bank loans finance does not come at the expense of anyone else's expenditure in the economy—as would be the case had the money been transferred. Thus bank lending leads to an increase in monetary expenditure at the aggregate level.

Chapter 9 also discussed how retentions in the flow of money between households and firms create recessionary forces: if the public does not spend, firms do not sell; if firms do not sell, they decide to produce less. It follows that bank lending unleashes forces working in the opposite direction—expansionary forces. By increasing the monetary expenditures of the public, bank lending tends to stimulate economic activity. When considering the consequences of such expansionary forces, however, we must be careful. Increasing monetary spending is not a free ticket to more production and lower unemployment—the results are not the mirror image of those observed when monetary spending decreases.

When the public spends less, firms can always react by decreasing production—all the way down to zero if the situation is dire enough. When the public spends more, firms can react by increasing their production—but only up to a certain limit. More production requires more resources—more labour, more machinery, more raw materials. If the economy finds itself in a state of "spare capacity"—if a substantial number of people are unemployed, machinery is not being used to its full potential, raw materials are available, and so on—then an increase in production is possible. If that is not the case, any given firm will only be able to increase its use of resources by attracting resources currently in use by other firms—thus reducing other firms' labour, capital, or raw materials. Aggregate production will not increase under such conditions, as the gain in the production of one firm will signify a loss in the production of some other. The economy would find itself at full capacity.

What happens when people have more money to spend but the economy is at full capacity? The answer is that prices start to increase. Firms trying to attract employees from other firms will offer higher wages, and the same goes for the price of inputs other than labour. Higher input prices are then passed on to consumers in the form of higher prices for the goods and services that firms sell. These higher prices, in turn, dilute the additional purchasing power gained by the public through money creation. An increase of monetary expenditures by 10% accompanied by an increase in consumption prices by 10% results in no change in the quantity of goods and services which the public can buy. Thus money creation by banks can have an expansionary effect, but only as long as the economy has spare capacity. Because most economies find themselves near full capacity most of the time, a substantial share of bank money creation leads to higher prices. Indeed, a small and positive rate of inflation is a typical feature of most modern economies.

Incidentally, the above explains why the savings which the public decides to keep in monetary form—and are therefore not transferred to others in the economy—do not result in recessions year after year. These savings have recessionary effects on their own, but they are more than compensated by new money entering the economy via bank lending. The money we put aside is dwarfed in magnitude by the additional money being created.

To summarize, bank lending has an expansionary effect on economic activity—it will stimulate production up to the point of full capacity, and lead to higher prices afterwards. But what of financial crises? The answer is that, so far, our analysis of the banking business has stopped at the point at which a loan is granted, disbursed, and spent. This, however, is only the first act in a relationship between bank and borrower which typically extends over a much longer period. Over the subsequent months and years, the borrower will make regular payments to the bank—to cover the interest due on the loan, and to repay the principal of the loan itself. These payments from borrower to bank will have consequences for the economy at large, and it is by considering them that we'll find our way into the logic of financial crises.

~~~

Interest payments are a transfer of money between agents in the economy. In accounting terms, the bank will debit a bank deposit in the name of the borrower and credit an account in its own name. This interest income is then used to pay for the bank's costs, such as salaries, and to produce a profit which is ultimately transferred to bank owners. To do so, the bank will debit the account where the interest income was first received and credit the bank deposits of its employees (in the case of salary payments) and those of bank owners (in the case of profit distribution). Thus, interest payments are nothing other than a transfer of bank deposits from the bank's borrowers to the bank's employees and owners.

The effect of any transfer of money on aggregate expenditures is, to a first approximation, zero. Consider, for instance, an interest payment of £1000 which you must make on your mortgage loan. These are £1000 which you no longer have at your disposal, and which will force you to reduce your expenditures in goods and services by, approximately, £1000. The money, however, has not leaked out of the system. Let us say the bank uses it to pay the wages of one of its employees. This employee will then go and spend his wages, approximately all of it, bringing the £1000 back into circulation and leaving aggregate expenditures unchanged.

A very different story results, however, from the second type of payment due to the bank: the reimbursement of the loan itself. Just like the granting of a bank loan does not involve a transfer of money from bank to borrower, reimbursing the loan does not involve a transfer of money from borrower back to the bank. Bank lending gives rise to money creation, and the reimbursement of a bank loan gives rise to the opposite phenomenon—money destruction.

When we pay back a bank loan, we instruct our bank to carry out the following two accounting operations. First, the bank debits a bank deposit in our name by the amount of our reimbursement. Second, the bank lowers the outstanding balance on our loan by this same amount. Since our bank deposit is a liability to the bank while our bank loan is an asset, both sides of the bank's balance sheet decrease by the same amount. The amount debited from our bank deposit is not transferred to anybody else in the economy—it simply ceases to exist.

Figure 11.1 presents the accounting entries on a bank's balance sheet over the whole lifecycle of a bank loan. Unlike figures from previous chapters, I present the balance sheet both before and after each of the actions considered has taken place—in order to highlight the changes.

In panel (a) Bank A grants a loan for a value of £100 to a borrower, and disburses the loan by issuing bank deposits. As we have seen in previous chapters, the balance sheet of the bank expands: a new bank loan is added to its assets side and a new bank deposit, in the name of the borrower, is added to its liabilities. In panel (b), the borrower spends the money—transferring the bank deposit received to a seller of goods and services. For simplicity, I assume this seller holds a bank account with the same bank as the borrower—nothing of substance would change if we were to introduce a second bank holding the seller's bank deposits, as we have done in previous chapters. When this payment is executed, Bank A debits the bank deposit of the borrower by £100 and credits the bank deposit of the seller by that same amount, leaving the total amount of bank liabilities unchanged.

We move on to panel (c), where the bank is ready to collect interest for a value of, let us say, £7. The action takes place sometime in the future, and the borrower has earned income from whatever economic activity he engages in. The borrower asks for some of this income to be paid as a credit into his bank deposit in Bank A, for a value of £7. Since the payment is made by a transfer from another bank, the operation results in a new debt in favour of Bank A and against another bank in the system, also for a value of £7. When interest is paid, Bank A simply debits the bank deposit of the borrower by the required amount. After passing through some intermediating accounts, the money is later credited as a bank deposit in the name of the bank's employees or owners—when salaries are paid and profits distributed. Total bank deposits thus remain unchanged.

Finally, panel (d) takes place at some point further in the future when the principal of the loan is due.[1] As before, the borrower arranges for some of the income he earns to be paid into his account at Bank A, this time for a value of £100. This is once again accompanied by an increase in the debts from other banks to Bank A, for that same value. When the time of repayment arrives, Bank A debits the bank deposit of the borrower by £100 and reduces the value of the bank loan outstanding all the way down to zero. Bank assets and bank liabilities decrease simultaneously and by the same amount, and nobody receives the money used to pay back the loan. The overall quantity of bank deposits in the economy has decreased by £100: money has been destroyed.

We are then, finally, able to state the core mechanism linking bank lending to the occurrence of financial crises. When banks make loans, they are not only creating money. Banks engage the economy into a cycle of monetary creation today followed by monetary destruction in the future (in addition to monetary transfers in between, in the form of interest payments). Monetary destruction has an unambiguous negative effect on aggregate expenditure. Consider, as we did before, a payment of £1000

---

[1] We assume the entire loan is due for repayment at a single point in time, but obviously the same conclusions follow when the loan is to be paid in multiple instalments.

Panel (a): Lending via bank deposit creation

Bank A

Bank Assets	Bank Liabilities

Bank A

Bank Assets	Bank Liabilities
Bank loan £100	Bank deposit of borrower £100

Panel (b): Spending of newly created bank deposit

Bank A

Bank Assets	Bank Liabilities
Bank loan £100	Bank deposit of borrower £100

Bank A

Bank Assets	Bank Liabilities
Bank loan £100	Bank deposit of borrower £0
	Bank deposit of seller £100

Panel (c): Payment of interest on loan

Bank A

Bank Assets	Bank Liabilities
Debts from other banks £7	Bank deposit of borrower £7
Bank loan £100	Bank deposit of seller £100

Bank A

Bank Assets	Bank Liabilities
Debts from other banks £7	Bank deposit of borrower £0
Bank loan £100	Bank deposits of employees and bank owners £7
	Bank deposit of seller £100

Panel (d): Repayment of the loan principal

Bank A

Bank Assets	Bank Liabilities
Debts from other banks £107	Bank deposit of borrower £100
Bank loan £100	Bank deposits of employees and bank owners £7
	Bank deposit of seller £100

Bank A

Bank Assets	Bank Liabilities
Debts from other banks £107	Bank deposit of borrower £0
Bank loan £0	Bank deposits of employees and bank owners £7
	Bank deposit of seller £100

Fig. 11.1 The complete life of a bank loan

to your bank—but this time for the purpose of repayment of the principal, rather than as interest on your loan. For you, nothing changes: these are still £1000 you no longer have at your disposal and which force you to reduce your expenses by, approximately, £1000. This time, however, the money you pay is not received by anybody. There is no accompanying increase in anybody else's expenditure across the economy, resulting in a net decrease in aggregate spending for, approximately, £1000. The action is detrimental to economic activity.

Under normal circumstances, the monetary destruction just described is more than compensated by money creation taking place at the same time. Banks make new loans as old loans are paid back, and the total value of loans outstanding typically grows from year to year. We have seen this in previous chapters, where figures showing the evolution of credit to the private sector is trending upwards most of the time. During typical years, then, the business of banking results in net monetary expansion and stimulates economic activity. The problem is, not all years have to be typical.

Financial crises are periods when new bank lending is severely curtailed or even comes to a halt, while repayments on existing loans continue. Loan repayments have been decided in advance—at any given point in time, the economy is committed to a certain path of monetary destruction. This is a central feature of all debt contracts: repayments are not contingent on the current economic environment, and there is no automatic mechanism for rescheduling them. A debtor must pay interest and principal as set initially, or else risk formal prosecution. New bank lending, on the other hand, can be as high or as low as banks and borrowers determine. If banks decide to rein in new lending to a substantial extent, they will inevitably force the economy into a deleveraging process.

When the economy is set into deleveraging mode, the machinery of economic recession is set into motion. Deleveraging implies monetary destruction, and monetary destruction implies reductions in aggregate expenditure. This acts as a brake on economic activity as firms will see their sales fall, which will lead them to produce less and lay off people. A series of additional reactions is then unleashed, all contributing to the severity of the problem. People who lose their job will be forced to reduce their expenditures. People who do not lose their job today but fear they may do so in the future will postpone large purchases and behave more thriftily. Firms, seeing the weakening demand, will stop new investment. Every one of these reactions further reduces expenditures, making matters worse. The recessionary forces unleashed by the deleveraging process are magnified and feed on each other. The larger the initial deleveraging, the more severe the ensuing recession.

If that was not bad enough, the negative developments just described are likely to be long-lasting. Debt deleveraging is the prime mover of the crisis and, since much debt is long term in nature, it may well remain in place for a number of years. If no other actors intervene in the drama, only a reversal of the deleveraging process will bring the crisis to an end. In other words, the crisis will stop when banks resume their lending which, in turn, will happen only once both banks and borrowers regain their confidence in the future prospects of the economy.

Previous chapters have highlighted the many benefits which an economy procures itself from banking activity. What we now see, however, is that banking also comes with certain risks attached. Bank lending makes the economy vulnerable to future monetary contraction, which in turn may cause a financial crisis. The larger the stock of bank loans, the larger the magnitude of loan repayments to which the public is engaged. If, for whatever reason, new bank lending slows down or comes to a halt, the consequences can be dire indeed.

Summing up, a financial crisis results when an economy builds up a stock of bank debt of substantial magnitude and subsequently sees new bank lending severely curtailed. Since existing loans must be repaid, the economy enters a period of debt deleveraging and monetary destruction, which pushes the economy into recession. This sequence of events matches well the pattern followed by credit over GDP in the years before and after the onset of a crisis—as illustrated by the study of crisis episodes in the preceding chapter. The question that remains to be answered, however, is why this happens. Why would banks and their borrowers behave in this way, accumulating debts at a frenetic pace at first, before reverting the trend and forcing themselves into deleveraging? Our understanding of financial crises will only be complete once we can answer this question.

CHAPTER 12

The Mechanics of Financial Crises—Part Two

Keywords Real estate · Mortgages · Speculation · Boom and bust · Investors' beliefs

The mechanism highlighted in the previous chapter applies to all forms of bank lending. Since all bank loans must be repaid in the future, they all give rise to monetary destruction and the potential to force reductions in aggregate expenditure. This may lead us to be suspicious of bank lending in general, and fear a constant recurrence of financial crises.

But such fears would be misguided. While individual banks may get in trouble with some frequency, system-wide financial crises are rare events, especially in wealthy economies. Over the 60-year period between 1945 and 2005 the majority of developed economies experienced no financial crisis whatsoever, while a handful of them experienced one episode.[1] The global financial crisis of 2008 changed this by hitting most of these economies simultaneously, but that still leaves a record of one major financial crisis in the 75 years up to 2020—hardly a recurrent pattern. While

---

[1] According to the most widely accepted classification of crisis episodes used in academic research, only Spain (1977), the United States (1988), Japan (1997) and Finland, Norway, and Sweden (1991) had a system-wide financial crisis during this period (Laeven & Valencia, 2018).

L. Angeles, *Money Matters*,
https://doi.org/10.1007/978-3-030-95516-8_12

complacency is not the order of the day, and steps should be taken to avoid a repeat of the 2008 episode, we should recognize that banks have been able to proceed with their business over several decades without regularly guiding the economy into widespread financial trouble.

Indeed, there are good reasons to believe that most forms of bank lending will not result in the rapid build-up of debts, and subsequent deleveraging, that brings about financial crises. Traditionally, banks have specialized in offering financing to firms, for the purpose of day-to-day purchases and long-term investment, and to households, for the purpose of consumption. As a rule, these forms of debt are not subject to sustained bursts of rapid growth since firms and households typically want to keep debt service in proportion to their incomes.

Take firms, for instance. As the economy grows firms will want to borrow more—for example, to finance the purchase of more raw materials to increase their production. A doubling of the economy, however, will typically lead to no more than a doubling of raw material purchases, and therefore to a doubling of bank finance—there is no runaway indebtment process but a growth in proportion to the growth of the economy. A similar argument can be made for households borrowing to finance consumption.

A financial crisis originating in traditional bank lending to firms and households is therefore highly unlikely. This debt does not explode in size, and the cost of servicing it, in the form of interest payments and reimbursement of the principal, tends to remain manageable. If that is the case, there will be no reason for banks to put a brake on their lending at some point in the future—they will simply lend each year a little more than last year, as their clients' income grows. With no eventual contraction of bank lending there is no shift towards deleveraging, and the mechanism of financial doom surveyed in the previous chapter will not be set in motion.

Financial crises, then, most likely stem from a third category of bank lending—a category for which the above rules do not seem to apply. Throughout the world, a major share of bank lending is used to finance neither firm investment nor household consumption, but the acquisition of real estate. Indeed, real estate purchases are typically made possible precisely by the granting of bank finance.

While banking is essential for the real estate market, the real estate market has also become pretty much essential for banks. Jorda, Schularick, and Taylor, whom we have encountered previously, have tracked the composition of bank lending in all major advanced economies from the late nineteenth century to the early twenty-first century. Their figures show that, as an average across all economies, lending for real estate purposes passed from 28% of all bank lending in 1928 to 38% in 1970—before rapidly accelerating to 55% of the total by the year 2007. In the United States, the epicentre of the global financial crisis, a whopping 70% of all bank lending was in the form of mortgages during the year 2007.[2]

Mortgages could be considered as just another instance of loans for consumption purposes when granted to households, and as loans for production purposes when granted to firms. After all, a house procures households with what economists call housing services, as essential an item of consumption as food or clothing. And buildings are part of the infrastructure that most firms need in order to operate. As long as households regard housing as consumption and firms regard buildings as business infrastructure, we have no reason to worry about mortgage lending. Households would budget their consumption of housing services in the same way they budget their consumption of everything else: in proportion to their total income. The same would apply to firms, who would expand their premises only as they expand their production levels. Mortgage lending of this type would not lead the economy into financial excess; it would accompany and assist the normal process of economic development.

But mortgage lending can also finance activity in the real estate market which is of a different nature altogether. Instead of buying houses in order to obtain housing services from them, households can buy them as a form of speculative investment. If house prices increase rapidly, the real estate market offers the opportunity to engage in the oldest form of get-rich-quick scheme: buy today, sell for a higher price tomorrow. What is more, because houses are bought using bank finance, the return on such investment may be increased several times over by leverage. Buying a house for £100,000 with your own money and selling it for £110,000 one year later is a 10% return on your investment. Buying that same house for £100,000, but this time using a bank loan to finance 95% of the purchase price plus £5000 of your own money, then selling it for £110,000 a year later, completely transforms the investment. Assume the bank loan is paid

---

[2] Jorda et al. (2016, p. 116).

back when the house is sold together with £4000 in interest due—that's a total payment to the bank of £99,000. That's still £11,000 earned from an initial investment of £5000—a rate of return of 120% over the course of a single year. No form of business investment can compete with this kind of return, and it certainly beats working for a salary.

Thus bank-financed speculation in the real estate market can be extremely lucrative and will attract a lot of people, but the link between this type of bank lending and financial crises does not derive from that fact. What makes mortgage lending for speculative purposes dangerous is that its size is not kept in line with the size of the overall economy. Mortgage loans are given as a proportion of the value of the property being purchased. Mortgage lending will therefore grow in proportion to real estate prices—if houses become twice as expensive, mortgages will be twice as large. And house prices need not grow in line with the rest of the economy—as our review of financial crisis episodes pointed out, house price growth can be many times larger than GDP growth, for several years in a row. If banks agree to keep financing real estate purchases as house prices soar, private sector indebtedness will deviate from long-term trends and become ever larger as a share of income. The service of such debt, then, will become ever more burdensome.

Households who purchase homes for the aim of living in them would be deterred from ever larger mortgages which engage an ever larger share of their income. But households who see homes as an investment opportunity will not. The reason can be observed in the calculations presented above. As long as house prices keep increasing, the gains from speculation will be large enough to pay the service of the debt and leave a substantial profit on top. Debt service growing as a proportion of your income does not matter if you don't expect to use your income to pay for it. And, together with this willingness to borrow, comes a willingness to lend from the part of the banks. Banks are not deterred from granting ever larger loans as long as the promise of house price rises ensures them the continuation of their interest income. Banks and bank borrowers, both stand to make a profit from the speculative venture.

Indeed, what makes financial crises particularly difficult to avoid, once a dynamic of rapidly increasing house prices is in place, is the fact that borrowers and banks are acting in a fully rational manner. Their activities are risky, but the profits they stand to make while the boom is ongoing more than compensate for the risk taken. The pressure to join in the activity will be substantial for households, who see friends and neighbours making big gains, but it is arguably even larger for banks. Households, after all, are free to stand aside and watch—but can bank managers do likewise? Most likely not, given that their jobs depend on their performance relative to their peers. As Charles Owen Prince, former chief executive of America's financial conglomerate Citigroup famously said while the crisis of 2008 was quickly unravelling, "[A]s long as the music is playing, you've got to get up and dance".[3] Bank lending and private indebtedness are bound to follow house prices in their road to ever more dizzying heights.

At some point, however, the music is going to stop and the boom in house prices is going to come to an end—it always does. I will say more about the reasons for this in a moment but, as house prices become more and more disconnected with the price of everything else, including average incomes across the economy, the confidence in their continuing rise eventually falters. Confidence counts for a lot in this game—not believing that house prices will keep increasing is the first step in them actually not increasing. And when house price growth slows down— let alone when house prices stop increasing and begin to decline—all hell breaks loose. Even with slowly increasing prices speculators will lose out: in the numerical example above, speculators break even with a 4% increase in house prices. Anything below that and they lose money. With stagnating or falling house prices speculators desert the market entirely and banks become weary of making mortgage loans to new customers. With mortgage lending being the most important component in banks' portfolios, new bank lending falls off a cliff. With few new loans forthcoming and old loans due for repayment, the economy enters into a forced deleveraging phase. As we have discussed already, recession and crisis ensue.

Thus mortgage lending for speculative investment can lead to a financial crisis if it expands rapidly as house prices soar and suddenly stops when the housing market turns sour. Debts are piled up during the boom period and their repayment after the bust leads to monetary destruction and lower aggregate expenditure—potentially for several years. At this point, only one question remains in place for us to understand the

---

[3] "Citigroup chief stays bullish on buy-outs", *The Financial Times*, 9 July 2007.

full dynamic of financial crises. The cycle of indebtedness and deleveraging will follow house prices, but why would house prices describe such a trajectory of boom and bust in the first place?

As it turns out, it is only when we consider the driving force behind house prices that the perversity of the whole scenario finally comes fully into view. Bank lending may be driven by house prices, but house prices themselves are driven by bank lending—there would be no boom in the real estate market if there was no accommodating mortgage provision in the first place. The vast majority of money used for real estate purchases is money just created by the banking system for that specific purpose. If banks were not willing to lend, real estate investors would not be able to outbid each other in the market and drive house prices upwards in the process. The boom is the outcome of a self-reinforcing circular mechanism. Banks create money that floods the real estate market because both banks and speculators expect to make profits thanks to rising house prices. And house prices do rise, driven precisely by the flood of new money into the real estate market. As long as banks and speculators believe in future price rises their belief will become true, as it will engender the actions that make it come about. As soon as they stop believing, the market will come down crashing.

And what makes market participants change their beliefs? The aftermath of all financial crises is characterized by much soul-searching, as analysts try to identify the one factor, or small group of factors, which triggered the downfall. A particular decision of the Central Bank, or some financial institution showing early signs of trouble, are common culprits. My message here is that such searches are of little use, as identifying one or a few triggers is of minor importance. House prices are bound to crash since they have become too out of line with other prices and incomes—people cease to believe they can keep rising, and that causes them to fall. The problem affecting the economy is the unsound nature of bank-financed speculation over a period of several years, which renders a turnaround increasingly inevitable. The trigger can be anything, and it is often an event which, under different circumstances, would have been negotiated by market participants with little inconvenience. Focusing on the trigger may detract us from the real causes of the crisis, which lie in the behaviour of banks and bank borrowers.

Boom and bust, then, are but two sides of the same coin—guided by the same underlying principles. Both reflect the logic of collective beliefs and herd behaviour, allied to the power of money creation and money destruction. If there is one difference between them, it is potentially in their speed. The boom is slower than the bust because people will keep a modicum of caution when following others in expectation of future gains. Such restraint is set aside when it comes to avoiding losses. When the time comes to reach for the door, it is always a stampede.

CHAPTER 13

Fighting Off Financial Crises

Keywords Monetary policy · Fiscal policy · Budget deficits ·
Government bonds · Central Banks · Fiscal austerity · The euro

When a financial crisis strikes, it is the responsibility of both the Central
Bank and the national government to counteract its effects and limit the
damage it causes. This they do, primarily, by acting on two policy levers:
monetary policy for the Central Bank, and fiscal policy for the national
government. This chapter assesses the usefulness of this policy response,
in the light of the mechanism put forward over the last two chapters.

Central Banks are usually the first to act—changes to monetary
policy can be decided and implemented in a matter of days if needed. As
we have seen previously, however, monetary policy is nothing other than
setting a target interest rate for the market of bank reserves. By lowering
this interest rate the Central Bank expects to stimulate the economy, as it
tends to make bank borrowing cheaper and may thus convince people to
borrow and spend more. In the aftermath of the global financial crisis of
2008, Central Banks across the world lost no time in pushing this rate as
low as it would go—all the way down to zero—and kept it there for as
long as the crisis lasted.

© The Author(s), under exclusive license to Springer Nature
Switzerland AG 2022
L. Angeles, *Money Matters*,
https://doi.org/10.1007/978-3-030-95516-8_13

Unfortunately, access to cheap bank reserves is of little use during major crisis episodes—the global financial crisis being a case in point. During that event, banks were reluctant to pass the lower rates they paid on their reserves onwards to their customers, as they perceived an increased risk of lending. Even more important, firms and households were not interested in borrowing, even if offered lower rates. Firms thought that prospects for business activity in the near future were dismal—investing in additional productive capacity was the last thing on their minds. Households feared for their capacity to service their existing debt—acquiring additional debt was out of the question. Somewhat better conditions on loans was never going to change this dynamic. Traditional monetary policy is therefore ineffective during severe financial crises. Accordingly, the rest of this chapter focuses on fiscal policy.

Fiscal policy may be defined as the use of taxation and government spending in order to influence the aggregate economy. Governments collect taxes from the public and use the proceeds to finance two types of expenditures. First, governments produce public goods and public services, or pay private firms to produce them on their behalf. Second, governments make welfare payments to large sections of the population—this includes unemployment benefits to people who have lost their job, and numerous forms of support to people with low incomes, disabilities, large families, etc.

The macroeconomic effects of fiscal policy derive from its capacity to increase aggregate expenditure. For this to happen, however, the government must run a budget deficit: its expenditures on goods and services plus the welfare payments it makes must exceed in value the receipts from taxation. Budget deficits are routinely reported in the media as a problem but, in the aftermath of a financial crisis, they are exactly what the economy needs.

A balanced government budget produces little or no change in aggregate expenditures. Tax payments reduce tax payers' disposable income, leading them to lower their expenditures on goods and services approximately by the amount paid in taxes. At the same time, the government uses the money received either to buy goods and services or to make welfare payments for people in need—who go on to spend the money received to buy goods and services. The increased expenditures of the state and welfare recipients compensate for the decreased expenditures of tax payers, leaving aggregate expenditures largely unchanged. Firms end up selling a larger share of their production to the state or to welfare recipients, rather than to the general public, but their overall sales do not change.[1]

Things are different with a budget deficit. Since the government cannot create money, it is forced to borrow the difference between the money it spends and the money it receives in taxes. This it does by issuing debts which we refer to as government bonds, and selling these to private agents against money in the form of bank deposits. The principal buyers of government bonds are pension funds and other private investors—in other words, we all finance the government deficit by buying government bonds with our savings.[2]

When governments run a budget deficit, then, they tap into our savings via borrowing instead of tapping into our income via taxation. Does this make a difference? The answer is that it may well do, if we consider that most income is destined to be spent, whereas a substantial amount of savings may not.

Under normal economic circumstances, we would worry that the government is simply redirecting towards itself some of the savings which the public uses to invest in the stock and bond markets—savings which were being transferred anyway, and would end up being spent by private agents in the economy. If that is the case, aggregate expenditures would remain unchanged: the government would be able to spend more, but only by forcing firms and households to spend less. Economists refer to this as the crowding-out effect: government spending crowds out private investment when both are tapping into the same source of money.

When the economy finds itself in a financial crisis, however, crowding-out becomes unlikely. Firms do not want to borrow given the poor prospects of the economy, while savers do not wish to lend to them because they perceive their debt as too risky. Indeed, financial markets during crisis periods are characterized by a so-called "flight to quality": investors move away from debt and equity instruments issued by private

---

[1] Of course, this is not saying that a balanced budget has no economic consequences. Poverty and inequality are greatly reduced by taxation and public spending, balanced budget or not.

[2] As noted earlier, government bonds are also bought by commercial banks, both as an investment vehicle and because they can be exchanged for additional bank reserves at the Central Bank.

firms and look for safer investment vehicles until the storm has passed. If no safe investment vehicles are available, investors would rather keep their savings in monetary form—money earns no income, but at least it is not subject to the risks of default or loss in value (like private debt and private equity, respectively).

It is at this point that government debt can play a crucial role. For reasons that we shall review shortly, bonds issued by the government of an advanced economy are typically considered risk-free—their probability of default is zero. Faced with the choice of keeping their savings in monetary form or buying government bonds instead, most people would choose the later: government bonds are as safe as currency, and pay a positive interest rate. Financial crises are therefore episodes in which government bonds are in high demand—so much so, indeed, that governments are able to pay ever smaller interest rates on their bonds and still have no difficulty in placing them. Take, for instance, the United Kingdom. Before the global financial crisis, between the years 2000 and 2008, the UK government had to pay an interest rate that fluctuated between 4 and 5.5% when borrowing from the market with a 10-year maturity. Once the crisis struck the interest rate on British debt falls swiftly: by the year 2012, the UK government was paying less than 2% on its 10-year bonds.[3] This, I note, took place despite a substantial increase in the quantity of government bonds issued. The UK government could expand its borrowing substantially and still see a decline in the rate it paid, so large was the increase in the demand for its bonds.

A budget deficit in times of crisis, then, is a very effective method to stimulate economic activity: it makes use of money which the public would have left out of circulation otherwise. Just as the public is setting money aside and intending not to make it available for private users, the government borrows the money and spends it. The decrease in private spending caused by the deleveraging process is therefore counteracted by an increase in public spending, reducing the recessionary forces acting on the economy.

This, however, is not the end of the story. While a budget deficit under crisis conditions is clearly beneficial, as long as the deficit is financed by

---

[3] Source: Federal Reserve Economic Data. https://fred.stlouisfed.org/series/IRLTLT 01GBM156N.

tapping into private savings it is unlikely to be large enough. Private savings are a limited resource and it may well be that, for a major crisis episode, they are not equal to the job.

~~~

When the global financial crisis struck back in 2008, nations across the developed world were spared the worst possible outcome thanks to a rapid shift towards large budget deficits. These deficits, however, were not the outcome of a conscious decision by governments to help a flailing economy. Instead, the deficits were caused by an automatic mechanism built into the institutional structure of these economies. Governments did not have to take any decision to put this mechanism in motion—thankfully for all of us.

When an economy enters into a period of recession, taxation and public expenditures change automatically, and in substantial amounts. Taxation falls, mainly because most taxes are in proportion to economic activity. Income tax is a share of our income, value added tax is a share of sales, and corporation tax is a share of firm profits. A recession lowers our incomes, sales and firm profits—it therefore lowers taxes. Public expenditures, on the other hand, increase—mainly because of welfare payments. Unemployment benefits rise as people lose their jobs, while falling incomes mean that more people qualify for other forms of welfare as well. With taxes falling and expenditures increasing a substantial budget deficit is bound to emerge—just in time, for that is what the economy needs.

Unfortunately, this automatic reaction will inevitably fall short of stopping a recession altogether—not by chance but by design. Unemployment benefits never fully compensate for the loss in wage income, while welfare benefits stop people from falling into indigence but do not ensure a living standard equal to the one enjoyed before crisis struck. There are arguably good reasons for this: people may adopt undesirable behaviours if losing a job had no consequence on their income. From a macroeconomic perspective, however, the implication is clear. The existence of these welfare programmes will avoid a complete collapse of spending for those who lose their jobs or experience economic hardship, but it will not maintain spending at its initial level. Welfare programmes will therefore lessen the effects of a financial crisis, but they will not eliminate them. To achieve that, governments would need to go beyond this automatic response.

Going beyond the automatic response means taking deliberate action to expand different forms of government spending. Governments can decide to invest in infrastructure projects such as roads or hospitals, hire more staff for social services, public health or education, or expand welfare programmes. This, however, is something that most governments across the world have been unwilling to do in the midst of a financial crisis. Indeed, such a course of action tends to be ruled out by the way in which budget deficits are perceived.

Budget deficits are universally regarded as a bad thing, and their existence is used to brand politicians as irresponsible, short-sighted, or incapable of financial planning. Budget deficits force the government to issue more debt, and the amount of public debt outstanding is often used as a measure to gauge the fiscal probity of governments. Worried for their reputation and electability, politicians tend to shy away from moves that would expand budget deficits boldly.

Such a deep-seated attitude may be of use when the economy finds itself at full employment, but proves to be a major handicap in times of financial crisis. Following the global financial crisis of 2008, and once the automatic reaction built into the system of taxation and welfare had done its job of keeping the economy afloat, most governments got busy trying to *reduce* public expenditures—too scared by the sight of rapidly rising debt levels. A decade of fiscal austerity thus followed. Like a sick person from whom the correct medicine is taken away too soon, economies across the Western world faltered and took quite longer than necessary to recover.

Why are public deficits so universally decried? The reasons stem not just from a lack of understanding of their role in supporting aggregate spending during recessions, but also from the notion that governments, like households, need to live within their means. Even those who admit that budget deficits would support the economy, often follow such admission by saying that, nevertheless, it would be irresponsible for the government to borrow excessively. The principle is often brandished with heavy moral overtones, as the undesirability of getting in debt is hammered into our heads from an early age. "Annual income twenty pounds, annual expenditure nineteen nineteen and six, result happiness. Annual income twenty pounds, annual expenditure twenty pounds ought and six, result misery" said Mr. Micawber to young David Copperfield in Dickens' classic.[4] The best advise for a person whose income does not cover his expenses is to reduce expenses, not to borrow the difference. Why would such a sound piece of advice not apply to government finances, as opposed to personal finances?

Because, in a nutshell, governments are not like people. When it comes to borrowing and paying back debt, they differ in two fundamental ways. First, a government never needs to repay its debt in full. This is because governments, unlike people, can be said to live forever—or, at any rate, for long enough to be always able to push debt further into the future. Governments can always refinance any debt that becomes due—unlike people, who are no longer able to do so once they reach the end of their income-earning life. Governments need not worry about paying back the principal on the public debt, they only need to worry about their capacity to service this debt. Public debt can be refinanced indefinitely, but the interest on this debt must be paid on a regular basis.

This, of course, is still constraining—there is only so much debt service that a government is able to cover given tax receipts and its commitments of public spending. Without any further considerations, the private sector would stop lending when public debt reaches a certain ceiling—determined by the government's ability to service this debt. Critics of public deficits often point this out as a reason for fiscal conservatism: the government cannot borrow beyond a certain point, even if it wanted. Here, however, is where governments differ from people in a second crucial way. As we have seen, modern governments cannot create money. What they can do, however, is set the policy objectives of the public institution with the capacity to do so, namely the Central Bank.

The Central Bank of every country is owned by its national government. This implies that any profit made by the Central Bank is paid to the government, and makes part of the government's income. This comes handy because the Central Bank makes profits by receiving interest payments on its assets—assets which are, for the most part, government bonds. A government reaching the limit of its debt service capacity has therefore a simple solution to this problem. It can persuade the Central

---

[4] That is, nineteen pounds nineteen shillings and six pence in the first case; twenty pounds zero shillings and six pence in the second case. Since there were twenty shillings in a pound and twelve pence in a shilling, misery would result from a deficit equal to one eight hundreth of our income.

Panel (a): Initial situation

Central Bank		Commercial Bank		Public	
Assets	*Liabilities*	*Assets*	*Liabilities*	*Assets*	*Liabilities*
				Government Bonds £100m	

Panel (b): Central Bank buys government bonds

Central Bank		Commercial Bank		Public	
Assets	*Liabilities*	*Assets*	*Liabilities*	*Assets*	*Liabilities*
Government Bonds £100m	Central Bank deposits £100m	Central Bank deposits £100m	Bank deposits £100m	Bank deposits £100m	

Fig. 13.1   How the Central Bank buys government bonds

Bank to increase its purchases of government bonds from the market—bonds which the government has issued previously to finance itself. Once this is done, debt service on those bonds will be due to the Central Bank which, when all is said and done, amounts to the government paying money to itself.

The Central Bank can always buy government bonds in any amount it wishes thanks to its capacity to issue Central Bank deposits at will. The process is slightly complicated by the fact that government bonds need to be bought from the public, and the public will only accept commercial bank deposits as payment (theoretically the Central Bank could pay using currency, but that would be hugely impractical given the sums involved). The Central Bank must therefore use commercial banks as buying agents, and does so by following the procedure outlined in Fig. 13.1.

Figure 13.1 reports the balance sheets of the three actors involved in this transaction: the Central Bank, a commercial bank, and the public. Panel (a) presents the initial situation where the public holds government bonds, which are an asset for it, for a value of £100 million. The bonds were issued previously by the central government in order to finance budget deficits. Panel (b) is where the action takes place. The Central

Bank decides to buy these bonds and asks the commercial bank to pay for them. The commercial bank does this by issuing new bank deposits in the name of the seller of government bonds—these bank deposits are a liability for the bank and an asset for the public. The government bond ceases to belong to the public and is now an asset of the Central Bank. To compensate the commercial bank, the Central Bank issues new Central Bank deposits—which are a liability for the Central Bank and an asset for the commercial bank. The balance sheets of the Central Bank and the commercial bank both expand by the same amount, which is the value of the government bonds being purchased, while the balance sheet of the public sees one asset exchanged for another one.

The operation in Fig. 13.1 creates money in the form of commercial bank deposits—£100 million worth of it. This creation of commercial bank deposits, in turn, relies on the Central Bank's capacity to issue its own deposits, which itself relies on the Central Bank's capacity to issue currency. Central Bank deposits are debts payable in currency; the Central Bank is able to issue them at will precisely because it can never run out of currency to pay for them. In this way, the government is able to reduce its debt against the public by, effectively, having the Central Bank create the money that pays for it.

Private investors recognize this reality. A country with a Central Bank capable of producing currency at will is also a country whose government will never default on its debt. This is why government bonds are considered risk-free, and private investors are eager to acquire them in times of crisis despite ever lower interest rates on them. Thus the idea that governments somehow cannot expand their budget deficits in times of crisis beyond a certain limit, and that the market might refuse to keep financing the government, is profoundly mistaken. As long as the Central Bank responds to the needs of society, as it must do if it is to fulfil its mandate, there is no limit to the budget deficit which the government can run—at any rate in nominal terms.

This, in turn, implies that a government can, if it so wishes, fully counteract the recessionary forces active during a financial crisis regardless of their size. Before I pointed out that this might not be feasible if governments can only mobilize savings set aside by the public. But Fig. 13.1 makes clear that government borrowing can exceed private savings by any amount whatsoever, by tapping into the money creation abilities of the Central Bank. Imagine, for instance, that the public has saved £100 billion which it wishes to use to buy government debt, while the government needs to borrow £200 billion to combat a crisis. The government would simply issue an initial batch of bonds worth £100 billion, sell it to the public, and ask the Central Bank to buy it from them. Since this replenishes the savings of the public, the government can then issue a second batch of bonds worth £100 billion, taking its deficit to the desired level.

This capacity of the government to issue debt, potentially in any amount, should be treated with caution. I am not at all suggesting that budget deficits are a solution for all the ills of an economy, or that a government should make systematic use of them outside financial crises. Budget deficits in periods of normal economic activity will redirect resources away from private investment—just like taxation redirects resources away from private consumption. There may be a justifiable case for doing so, but it needs to be looked at carefully. As an example, consider the construction of a bridge when the economy is at full employment. The bridge may be a desirable addition to the country's infrastructure or it may not, but in all cases the workers and the construction equipment required would have been made unavailable for private construction projects, such as residential buildings.

In times of financial crisis, however, matters are quite different. Government deficits then are not only feasible, but highly desirable: they bring aggregate spending back to the level required for full employment. Consider once again the construction of a bridge, but this time when the economy is in a recession, large numbers of construction workers are without a job, and machinery lays unused. Thanks to deficit spending, not only will a bridge get built: unemployed people will be given a job, the economy will be stimulated by these people's income, and no private construction projects will be disadvantaged in the process. What's not to like?

~~~

So far I have argued that fiscal policy is an effective tool for fighting off an ongoing financial crisis—a tool that governments, sadly, fail to use to the extent that is needed. For anyone familiar with the finance pages of major newspapers, however, some of the assertions I have made must have appeared mystifying. Are governments really capable of borrowing any amount they want? Aren't governments forced to pay higher interest rates on their debts in times of crisis? What about Greece, or Italy, or

Spain, in the decade or so after 2008? What about Argentina, or Mexico, or Russia, all along the twentieth century? No one vaguely familiar with the experience of these countries would ever make the claims I have made about government finances.

Indeed. But further analysis of the cases just mentioned only confirms my assertions—provided we recognize how the conditions under which these countries operate differ from those considered so far. Up to this point, I have assumed we are dealing with countries where: (a) The government issues bonds denominated in the country's own currency, and (b) The Central Bank has the capacity to produce said currency at will. If either of these two conditions does not hold, the capacity to finance government deficits changes radically.

Governments from developing countries have a long history of getting in trouble with their creditors, often international banks based in developed economies. Why so? Because they fail to satisfy condition (a) above: they are forced to issue debts denominated in a foreign currency— American dollars, British pounds, or European euros. Since their Central Banks do not have the capacity to issue Central Bank deposits denominated in those currencies, they cannot buy this debt back. These governments are therefore treated much like common debtors: there is a limit to how much they can borrow and, as that limit is approached, creditors demand additional guarantees and charge a higher interest rate. Some of the most dramatic episodes of international finance over the last two centuries have taken place when countries in such a position have refused to keep servicing their debt. The reason why developing countries borrow in foreign currencies, in turn, is quite simple. Only a handful of currencies are accepted by investors and financial institutions across the world. Investors will lend in a currency they trust, or not lend at all.

Until the end of the twentieth century, the above situation was believed to characterize developing countries only. The twenty-first century, however, brought to us a monetary experiment unprecedented in human history which, unbeknown to its designers, put a number of advanced economies into a comparable situation. On the first of January 1999, a group of eleven European nations launches the euro—the first time that a collection of independent nations decides to relinquish their national currencies and adopt a common one. Much was said at the time, and continued to be said afterwards, about the benefits and disadvantages of the new currency. Its proponents said it facilitated trade, tourism, and the circulation of workers and capital; and that it made possible the creation of a pan-European market. Its detractors pointed out that it forced a single monetary policy stance on the whole continent—in other words, that any interest rate on bank reserves would inevitably be too high for some countries and too low for others. Both sides had a point, albeit the quantitative importance of the alleged effects still awaits demonstration.

What neither proponents nor detractors seemed to emphasize, however, was that the introduction of the euro invalidated condition (b) above. Euros were to be produced by the European Central Bank, a new institution which did not answer to any individual national government. The Central Banks of European countries in the Eurozone continued to exist, but they lost the capacity to produce their countries' currency.

When discussed, this untested institutional structure was regarded as an advantage: all governments had to rely on fiscal discipline to balance their books, no recourse to Central Bank help was possible. The principle may have merit under normal economic circumstances, but was to prove fatal under financial crisis conditions. The euro seemed to be designed for a set of economies that would never experience financial mayhem—a massive miscalculation.

As we know all too well, Eurozone countries were hit by the global financial crisis only nine years into the life of the euro. The crisis did what all such crises do: force governments into a budget deficit because of decreasing tax incomes and increasing welfare payments. The deficits had to be maintained, and ideally expanded, in order to fight off the crisis. This time, however, European governments could not count with the full support of a Central Bank to achieve this aim. The European Central Bank was notoriously reluctant to expand purchases of government bonds, eventually doing so much later and with less conviction than Central Banks in other advanced nations. Clearly, Eurozone countries did not have the same monetary leeway as countries such as the United Kingdom, the United States, or Japan did, and financial markets treated them accordingly.

Some European nations entered the global financial crisis with low levels of public debt and a reputation for fiscal probity—Germany, Austria, the Netherlands. These countries found it easy to finance their budget deficits at low interest rates and, because of that, could sustain their economies adequately throughout the crisis. Other nations entered the crisis with high levels of public debt and/or a reputation for lack of fiscal discipline—Italy, Spain, and, more than any other European nation, Greece. These countries found that investors were reluctant to keep financing their deficits, and charged an increasing interest rate to do so—a predicament normally associated with countries outside Western Europe. With no good options on the table, countries of the European south forced themselves into reducing public expenditures and welfare payments in the midst of a financial crisis of the most severe kind—with predictable consequences. For a sobering look at what can befall to a country that loses its monetary sovereignty, we only need to look at Greece.

The unemployment rate in Greece, which stood at 8% of the labour force when the crisis struck, rapidly increases and remains above 20% between late 2011 and early 2018, reaching a peak of 27% during 2013—fully comparable with the Great Depression. There is simply no chance that such an economic disaster would have been allowed to take place had Greece been indebted in its own currency, with a Central Bank capable of producing it. None of this is to deny that Greece's public finances were not in order, and that adjustments were long overdue. But the amount of economic suffering imposed on its population was not only very great but, for the most part, quite perfectly avoidable.

Fiscal policy is our first line of defence when facing recessions of any kind, and should be used fearlessly by governments who understand the logic of the intervention they are performing. The operation of fiscal policy, however, does not rely solely on the actions of a central government. The existence of a Central Bank with the capacity to buy government debt via money creation is crucial, and its absence can render fiscal policy unfeasible. The experience of countries in the European south should be studied and understood by any nation contemplating the abandonment of its capacity to create its own currency.

Before moving on, let us close this chapter by considering methods to fight off financial crises which lie beyond the usual policy spectrum. While fiscal policy counteracts the fall in private expenditure by expanding public expenditure, a more direct approach would stop private expenditure from falling in the first place.

Stopping the fall in private expenditure could be achieved by addressing its underlying cause: debt deleveraging. In other words, the private sector could be spared from the necessity of paying off existing debts—at least for the time being. The move would stop money from being destroyed, keeping it in the hands of firms and households who would be able to use it to maintain their spending at normal levels.

The least disruptive way to achieve this aim would involve commercial banks voluntarily granting payment holidays, extending loan maturities, reducing the interest rate, and even writing off part of the debts due to them. Debt repayments would be set to resume as economic activity recovers. Governments could play a role supporting the banks' actions, for instance by having the Central Bank granting them loans on soft terms, or adding to their capital. If this course of action is not feasible, a more active policy stance would be for the Central Bank to simply buy the debt owed by the public. The Central Bank would pay for this by issuing Central Bank deposits, in the manner we have seen before. Once this is done, bank debtors become debtors to the Central Bank, who can then soften the conditions on their loans by following any or all of the policies just mentioned.

Buying private debt and restructuring its payments, or even cancelling some of the amount due, amounts to using Central Bank money creation to partially bail out private debtors. The policy would need to be targeted well to gain acceptance from the general public. Debt relief should not be directed to those who stood to gain from real estate speculation, but to those who became indebted as a result of normal life circumstances and whose capacity to pay back debt suffered as a consequence of the crisis. In this, as in all matters, the government must act with fairness and probity for its actions to be regarded as legitimate.

CHAPTER 14

Preventing Financial Crises

Keywords Bank capital · Loan defaults · Bank lending · Real estate

Fighting off an ongoing financial crisis is important, but we'd much rather not have the crisis in the first place. Prevention of future crises has been high on the policy agenda since the events of 2008, but the way policy makers have gone about it reveals their misconceptions about why this crisis took place, and what would take to prevent a new one.

One of the most visible symptoms of a financial crisis is trouble in the banking sector: commercial banks experience default rates on their loans several times larger than during business as usual. This is especially true following a period of debt-financed speculation in the real estate market, as debtors often do not have the means to service their debt and rely on continuing growth in house prices to be able to do so. When a bank loan is in default status, banks write it off, either in part or entirely, from the assets side of their balance sheet. The corresponding change on the liabilities side is a decrease in bank capital, which may be understood as a non-refundable loan from the bank owners to the bank. Unlike normal loans, the value of bank capital is variable: it is defined as the value of all bank assets minus the value of all bank liabilities. Loan defaults decrease the value of bank assets, and therefore lower bank capital.

L. Angeles, *Money Matters*,
https://doi.org/10.1007/978-3-030-95516-8_14

If loan defaults are large enough bank capital can become negative—at which point the bank is classified as insolvent (in other words, it would not be able to pay off its debts even when liquidating all its assets). A bank in such a state will not retain the trust of its creditors, and will soon be forced into bankruptcy.

In the aftermath of the global financial crisis of 2008, with banks fully exposed to losses on their mortgage portfolios, governments went to extraordinary lengths to prevent insolvencies and bank failures. To maintain the trust of bank creditors, governments expanded the amounts covered by existing deposit insurance schemes and extended guarantees on bank liabilities other than bank deposits. They made capital injections into banks suffering large losses on their loans, and into banks with low levels of capital. They facilitated the acquisition of poorly capitalized banks by well-capitalized banks, often by buying the worse part of the asset portfolio of the bank in trouble—and suffering the resulting losses. When everything else failed governments took over some banks themselves, managed them for a number of years, and returned them into private ownership once the crisis abated. As a result of all this, the banking infrastructure of most advanced economies survived very well throughout the crisis. Banks stood ready to continue their role of financing households and firms, once the demand for bank lending eventually returned.

Most of what is understood as prevention policy in this context has been designed with the above events in mind. By and large, governments have focused on making banks more resilient to future losses on their asset portfolios—something that can be achieved by strengthening capital requirements. If, before the global financial crisis, banks would have been allowed to hold capital for a value of only 5% of their assets, that would no longer do. A higher ratio would henceforth be required. More capital implies that banks are more likely to endure a future crisis without recourse to public funds. Because holding more capital is costly, the change forces bank owners to assume the cost of making their business more secure—instead of passing that cost to the state. This is surely an improvement on the status quo.

What larger capital requirements will not do, however, is prevent a financial crisis from taking place. Avoiding bank failures, or avoiding banks from requiring public assistance, is not the same as avoiding a crisis. A well-capitalized bank is just as likely to finance asset market speculation as a poorly capitalized one—perhaps more so, if the larger capital cushion leads it to think it can incur larger risks. And once the speculative boom turns into a bust, debt deleveraging will take over whether banks are well capitalized or not. Nothing in the mechanism explaining financial crises suggests that a different course will be taken if banks hold more capital.

Effective financial crisis prevention requires a correct understanding of how financial crises work, so that policies aimed at its underlying causes can be designed and implemented. To prevent financial crises, governments and Central Banks have no option but to look right into the bank lending business, taking actions to discourage the parts of it which are fuelling excessive speculative activity.

This last point is crucial, for it implies that traditional monetary policy is far too blunt to be useful. Monetary policy changes the interest rate on bank reserves, rendering bank lending more or less costly across the board. But across the board is precisely what we don't want, for much of bank lending is beneficial to society and does not lead to financial crises. Even worse, rising interest rates are likely to have a more discouraging effect on the forms of bank lending we would like to retain and encourage, and less on those we would like to avoid. Imagine that, following a change in monetary policy, bank lending rates increase to 8% for all types of loans. This rate will stop all investment projects with an expected rate of return below 8% from taking place. Most business investments may fall below this mark, but not so speculative investments in the real estate market which, as we have seen, can be hugely profitable under rapid house price growth. It is therefore unlikely that speculators will be deterred by the rise in interest rates.

What financial regulators need to do, then, is adopt policies that limit bank lending for specific purposes, rather than across the board. Bank lending for business investment and bank lending to finance household consumption are usually not a danger, and could be left largely unmolested. It is only bank lending for the purpose of asset market transactions, in particular real estate purchases, that needs to be closely monitored and, on occasion, curtailed. This calls for a far more interventionist policy stance than what has been the usual practice over the last few decades.

The specific policy interventions that could be implemented are many. I mention a few ones, purely for illustrative purposes. The government could tax mortgages for the purchase of property other than a primary family residence, making them less attractive. Or it could impose a higher capital gains tax on property sales if the property has been owned for less than a specific period of time, or not been used by its owner. Or it could simply impose tighter limits on the amount people can borrow for mortgage purposes, reducing the number of times people can borrow their own annual income. What is more, the government would ideally make many of these interventions contingent on the state of the real estate market. Restrictions could be eased when house prices are increasing in line with inflation, and would be tightened when they exceed inflation by a significant amount.

While the specific policy mix that would give best results is not clear, the overall policy direction is clear enough—which, ultimately, seems to be the problem. Financial liberalization was adopted during the 1980s and 1990s under the general presumption that leaving banks alone to do their work is the best possible policy. This view has largely continued to dominate policy circles upto the present day.

Empirical evidence and better theory, however, should lead us to reappraise the issue. On the empirical side, a tendency for large financial crises to follow liberalization episodes has long been noted in the literature (and was highlighted in Chapter 10 of the present work). And while theory has often been brandished in favour of financial liberalization, the underlying arguments have typically relied on a traditional view of the banking business. According to this view, banks are institutions financing the productive investment of firms, and they do so by transferring funds which have been provided to them by the public. It would be in the banks' own best interest to allocate these funds to their most productive uses, and the state can only hamper the process by getting in the way.

As we have seen at different stages all along this book, however, this traditional view of banks is deficient in two fundamental ways. First, banks do not merely allocate funds, they create the funds to be allocated. This is crucial because money creation when debt is granted comes hand in hand with money destruction when debt is paid back, which means that large stocks of bank debt carry the risk of financial crisis if unsustainable. And second, banks do not only finance productive investment by firms. An increasingly large share of the banking business is dedicated to the purchase of real estate, which can easily turn into financial speculation. This form of investment is unsustainable, as its success depends on the continuing provision of more bank debt. Put these two elements together and the case for increased government intervention in the banking business becomes rather convincing.

The future occurrence of financial crises, then, depends on our ability to diagnose their causes correctly. The resilience and stability of our financial architecture has been improved in the past—let us recall that bank runs were once seen as inherent to the banking business, and are now a distant memory in most countries all around the world. Financial crises may well go the same way, provided we are open-minded enough to question long-standing views, revise our understanding, and act accordingly.

FURTHER READING

I have addressed many topics covered in this book in some of my academic work. On the business of modern banking see Angeles (2019), on the history of money see Angeles (2020).

The literature on the history of money and banking is vast, and only rarely makes a clear distinction between modern banking (via bank deposit creation) and ancient banking (via currency transfer). With this caveat in mind, there is much to learn from this literature and I can recommend the following.

A good overview of the history of money from its earliest beginnings to the present day is offered by Davies (2002). Goetzmann (2016) is an engaging account of financial innovations—not limited to money and banks—all along human history. Martin (2014) is a history of money for the general public packed with interesting facts and engaging commentary. Finally, for a history of monetary developments in the United States which proves that scholarly work can be readable and entertaining, it would be difficult to do better than Galbraith (1975).

Graeber (2012) is quite unique and worth the effort, offering a universal history of debt from an anthropological perspective. Grierson (1977) also touches on anthropology, as well as history, in discussing the origins of money.

For money in antiquity, Von Reden (2010) is a great resource. Schaps (2004) tells the story of the invention of coinage and its adoption in ancient Greece perhaps better than anyone else. Von Reden (2007) covers

© The Author(s), under exclusive license to Springer Nature Switzerland AG 2022
L. Angeles, *Money Matters*,
https://doi.org/10.1007/978-3-030-95516-8

the case of Ptolemaic Egypt in detail, and Harris (2008) that of ancient Rome.

For coinage during the Middle Ages, the reader should consult Spufford (1989). For more discussion on coinage debasement I recommend Munro (2012) and Rolnick et al. (1996).

On the history of banking from its earliest beginnings to the twentieth century, the best reference by far is Bogaert et al. (1994)—a work which is not only well written, but also very impressively illustrated. Those with a specific interest in banking during Roman times can turn to Andreau (1999).

The origins of lending by bank deposit creation are discussed by Usher (1934), De Roover (1974), and, more recently, Geva (2011).

The history of public banks is surveyed masterfully by Roberds and Velde (2016). On the founding of the Bank of England and the development of modern banknotes, Desan (2014) is excellent. Horsefield (1960) may also be consulted to understand the context better.

On how Central Banks evolved over time, Goodhart (1988) is full of insights and Kindleberger (1993) gives the context. For how Central Banks carry out monetary policy in practice, Bindseil (2004) is the best resource.

On the abandonment of gold convertibility, I recommend Redish (1993) and, again, Galbraith (1975).

On financial crises, a huge and active academic literature is in place— I have referred to some of this work in the main text. There are also numerous book treatments for the general public, but these differ in quality. Two that I am happy to recommend are Turner (2016) and King (2016).

Finally, for works emphasizing the limitations of how money and banking are typically portrayed in economics the reader may consult Ingham (2004) and Wray (2004), plus a number of academic papers by Charles Goodhart—including Goodhart (1998, 2007, 2017). Goodhart (1998) also contains a discussion of potential future problems with the euro which is the most impressive act of economic foresight I have ever witnessed.

References

Andreau, J. (1999). *Banking and business in the Roman world*. Cambridge University Press.

Angeles, L. (2019). On the Nature of Banks, Kyklos. *International Review for Social Sciences, 72*(3), 381–399.

Angeles, L. (2020). *Four phases in the history of money* (Adam Smith Business School Discussion Paper 2020–24), University of Glasgow.

Benston, G. J. (1983, March). Deposit insurance and bank failures, economic review. *Federal Reserve Bank of Atlanta, 68*, 4–17.

Bindseil, U. (2004). *Monetary policy implementation: Theory, past, and present.* Oxford University Press.

Bogaert, R., Kurgan-van Hentenryk, G., & van der Wee, H. (1994). *A history of European banking.* Fonds Mercator Paribas.

Dalton, G. (1982). Barter. *Journal of Economic Issues, 16*, 181–190.

Davies, G. (2002). *A history of money: From ancient times to the present day.* University of Wales Press.

Dell'Ariccia, G., Igan, D., Laeven, L., & Tong, H. (2016). Credit booms and macrofinancial stability. *Economic Policy, 2016*, 299–357.

De Roover, R. (1974). *Business, banking, and economic thought in late medieval and early modern Europe.* The University of Chicago Press.

Desan, M. (2014). *Making money: Coin, currency, and the coming of Capitalism.* Oxford University Press.

Drees, B., & Pazarbasioglu, C. (1998). *The Nordic banking crises: Pitfalls in financial liberalization?* (International Monetary Fund Occasional Paper No. 161).

Galbraith, J. K. (1975). *Money: Whence it came, where it went.* Andre Deutsch.

© The Author(s), under exclusive license to Springer Nature Switzerland AG 2022
L. Angeles, *Money Matters*,
https://doi.org/10.1007/978-3-030-95516-8

Galbraith, J. K. (1987). *A history of economics: The past as the present*. Penguin Books.

Geva, B. (2011). *The payment order of antiquity and the middle ages: A legal history*. Hart Publishing.

Goetzmann, W. N. (2016). *Money changes everything*. Princeton University Press.

Goodhart, C. A. E. (1988). *The evolution of Central Banks*. The MIT Press.

Goodhart, C. A. E. (1998). The two concepts of money: implications for the analysis of optimal currency areas. *European Journal of Political Economy, 14*, 407–432.

Goodhart, C. A. E. (2007). The continuing muddles of monetary theory: A steadfast refusal to face facts. *Economica, 76*(Supplement 1), 821–830.

Goodhart, C. A. E. (2017). The determination of the money supply: Flexibility versus control. *The Manchester School, 85*(S1), 33–56.

Graeber, D. (2012). *Debt: The first 5000 years*. New York: Melville House.

Grierson, P. (1977). *The origins of money*. The Athlone Press.

Harris, W. V. (2008). The nature of Roman money. In W. V. Harris (Ed.), *The monetary systems of the Greeks and Romans*. Oxford University Press.

Horsefield, J. K. (1960). *British monetary experiments 1650–1710*. Bell for the London School of Economics.

Humphrey, C. (1985). Barter and economic disintegration. *Man, 20*(1), 48–72.

Ingham, G. (2004). *The nature of money*. Polity Press.

International Monetary Fund (IMF). (2012, April). Dealing with Household Debt, Chapter 3 in World Economic Outlook.

International Monetary Fund (IMF). (2017, October). Household debt and financial stability, Chapter 2 in Global Financial Stability Report.

Jorda, O., Schularick, M., & Taylor, A. M. (2013). When credit bites back. *Journal of Money, Credit, and Banking, 45*, 3–28.

Jorda, O., Schularick, M., & Taylor, A. M. (2016). The great mortgaging: Housing finance, crises and business cycles. *Economic Policy, 2016*, 107–152.

Kadens, E. (2015). Pre-modern credit networks and the limits of reputation. *Iowa Law Review, 100*, 2429–2455.

Keynes, J. M. (1930 [reprinted 1971]). *A treatise on money: The collected writings of John Maynard Keynes* (Vol. V). The Macmillan Press.

Kindleberger, C. P. (1993). *A financial history of Western Europe* (2nd ed.). Oxford University Press.

King, M. (2016). *The end of alchemy: Money, banking and the future of the global economy*. Little, Brown.

Koo, R. (2008). *The holy grail of macroeconomics: Lessons from Japan's Great recession*. Wiley.

Laeven, L., & Valencia, F. (2018). *Systemic banking crises revisited* (IMF working paper 18/206).

Martin, F. (2014). *Money: The unauthorised biography*. Vintage.

McCloskey, D. N. (2019). *Why liberalism Works.* Yale University Press.

Mian, A., & Sufi, A. (2010). Household leverage and the recession of 2007 to 2009. *IMF Economic Review, 58,* 74–117.

Mian, A., Sufi, A., & Verner, E. (2017). Household debt and business cycles worldwide. *Quarterly Journal of Economics, 132*(4), 1755–1817.

Mill, J. S. (1848). *Principles of political economy* (Vol. II, Book III, Chapter VII). John W. Parker.

Muldrew, C. (1998). *The economy of obligation.* Macmillan Press.

Munro, J. H. (2012). The technology and economics of coinage debasements in Medieval and Early Modern Europe: With special reference to the Low Countries and England. In J. H. Munro (Ed.), *Money in the pre-industrial world: Bullion, debasements and coin substitutes.* Pickering & Chatto.

Ranciere, R., Tornell, A., & Westermann, F. (2006). Decomposing the effects of financial liberalization: Crises vs. growth. *Journal of Banking and Finance, 30,* 3331–3348.

Redish, A. (1993). Anchors Aweigh: The transition from commodity money to fiat money in western economies. *Canadian Journal of Economics, 26*(4), 777–795.

Roberds, W., & Velde, F. R. (2016). The descent of central banks (1400–1815). In M. D. Bordo, O. Eithheim, M. Flandreau, & J. F. Qvigstad (Eds.), *Central banks at a crossroads.* Cambridge University Press.

Rolnick, A. J., Velde, F. R., & Weber, W. E. (1996). The debasement puzzle: An essay on medieval monetary history. *The Journal of Economic History, 56*(4), 789–808.

Schularick, M., & Taylor, A. M. (2012). Credit booms gone bust: Monetary policy, leverage cycles, and financial crises, 1870–2008. *American Economic Review, 102*(2), 1029–1061.

Schumpeter, J. A. (1954). *History of economic analysis.* Allen & Unwin.

Smith, A. (1776 [reprinted 1976]). *An inquiry into the nature and causes of the wealth of nations.* University of Chicago Press.

Spufford, P. (1989). *Money and its use in medieval Europe.* Cambridge University Press.

Schaps, D. M. (2004). *The invention of coinage and the monetization of ancient Greece.* University of Michigan Press.

Turner, A. (2016). *Between debt and the devil: Money, credit, and fixing global finance.* Princeton University Press.

Usher, A. P. (1934). The origins of banking: The primitive bank of deposit, 1200–1600. *The Economic History Review, 4*(4), 399–428.

Van de Mieroop, M. (2002). Credit as a facilitator of exchange in Old Babylonian Mesopotamia. In M. Hudson & M. van de Mieroop (Eds.), *Debt and economic renewal in the ancient Near East.* CDL.

Von Reden, S. (1995). *Exchange in ancient Greece.* Duckworth.

Von Reden, S. (2007). *Money in Ptolemaic Egypt*. Cambridge University Press.

Von Reden, S. (2010). *Money in classical antiquity*. Cambridge University Press.

Wray, L. R. (Ed.). (2004). *Credit and state theories of money: The contributions of A. Mitchell Innes*. Edward Elgar.

INDEX

Printed in the USA
CPSIA information can be obtained
at www.ICGtesting.com
LVHW021323091223
765943LV00006B/342